Mrs. W.W. Charters

— with deepest respect
and affection — and
the grateful remembrance
of inspiring association
with Dr. Charters and
yourself — Sincerely
Lew Morrill

9/14/60

# THE ONGOING STATE UNIVERSITY

# THE ONGOING STATE UNIVERSITY

## James Lewis Morrill

THE UNIVERSITY OF MINNESOTA PRESS
*Minneapolis*

PRINTED IN THE UNITED STATES OF AMERICA AT THE
NORTH CENTRAL PUBLISHING COMPANY, ST. PAUL

*Library of Congress Catalog Card Number: 60-9636*

PUBLISHED IN GREAT BRITAIN, INDIA, AND PAKISTAN BY THE OXFORD UNIVERSITY PRESS,
LONDON, BOMBAY, AND KARACHI, AND IN CANADA BY THOMAS ALLEN, LTD., TORONTO

WE ARE GRATEFUL to the publishers for permission to use here materials revised and adapted from papers by James Lewis Morrill that first appeared in the following: *Addresses and Proceedings of the 75th Anniversary of the State University* (Ohio State University Press, 1951); American Alumni Council, *News* (October 1949) and *Report of the 34th National Conference, July 11–14, 1949*; *Annals of the American Academy of Political and Social Science* (September 1955); Association of Land-Grant Colleges and Universities, *Proceedings of the 62nd Annual Convention, November 11–12, 1948*; *Athletic Journal* (February 1947); *Bulletin of the American Institute of Banking* (July 1950); *Commemorative Papers from the Iowa State College Centennial, Founder's Day Convocation, May 22, 1958* (Iowa State University Press, 1958); *Functions of a Modern University* (State University of New York, 1950); *Journal of Health, Physical Education, Recreation* (February 1948); National Association of State Universities, *Proceedings* (May 2–3, 1955, and May 5–6, 1958); National Collegiate Athletic Association, *Proceedings of the 41st Annual Convention, January 7–8, 1947*; *Proceedings and Inauguration of Gordon Gray as President of the Consolidated Universities of North Carolina, October 8–10, 1950*; *Vital Speeches of the Day* (November 15, 1954).

# *Preface*

To ATTEMPT some interpretation of "the ongoing state university" is a difficult endeavor. The "tradition" of the state university is too recent and too young. Its mission is still undefined and empirical in our changing society, despite its significant and substantial history.

For one thing, the institution is more a "multiversity" than a "university" in the older and simpler sense of the word. Scholars and philosophers have long struggled and still struggle to make articulate "the idea of a university." José Ortega y Gasset's profoundly insightful summons is infinitely inspiring. Farthest from his thought was any intention to define the mission of the modern American state university, we know; and yet we do strive to respond to his challenge that "the university must be open to the whole reality of its time" — that "it must be in the midst of real life, and saturated with it," that "the life of the people needs acutely to have the university participate, *as* the university, in its affairs."

This transcendent challenge intuitively all of us who serve in universities understand in varying ways and degrees. The true scholar comprehends and responds to it best in the realms of the humanities and the social sciences and of basic research for the advancement of learning and the search for truth in every discipline. The university administrator shares, too, in this response.

Like politics, university administration is also the art of the possible, of helping to make possible the aims of both the philosophical and the practical as scholarship and science and society are able to perceive and conceive these aims.

Too little, I am aware, these chapters make plain this large responsibility. The world of current administrative perplexities is too much in them. But "the present contains all that there is," as Whitehead wrote. Not literally all that there is, for it must comprehend the past and the future as well, as he said — but the present is all that we have to work with. It is the problems and pressures of the present and their longer range implications with which the university administrator must deal — and deal today with whatever wisdom and discernment he can muster.

"He must preside at commencements, alumni dinners, educational conventions, conclaves of a dozen varieties of visiting firemen, and make at least one speech a week," Hans Zinsser wrote, describing the almost impossible plight of the American college president with amazing and amusing insight in his biography of "R. S.," *As I Remember Him.* His fuller description has comforted me, and hosts of my harassed presidential colleagues also, I surmise.

And so college presidents must make speeches. This volume brings together many of my own — an editorial selection and adaptation of things thought and said during the fifteen years of my participation in the ongoing of a productive institution, the University of Minnesota.

This editorial adaptation, the work of Mrs. Peggy Harding Love, has been accomplished with remarkable skill — and most appreciatively let me acknowledge my indebtedness to her. No one chapter of this book represents a single address of mine. Each chapter comprises selections from many different manuscripts. To bring these into some kind of perspective, appropriate to the chapter heading, must have been no easy task.

Few university presidents have reliance upon a "ghost writer" — and certainly not I. But most of us have relied often upon colleagues of our faculties and staffs, in varying degree, for helpful fact-finding, for scholarly backgrounding, and sometimes for re-sourceful ideas relevant to our themes. It is impossible, I regret, to name and thank all who so generously have helped me from time to time — but many of them will recognize their anonymous partnership with the author of this compendium and will know of my gratitude for indispensable assistance.

There is an inevitable redundancy in the volume — but one arising from convictions deeply held and often re-expressed in varied contexts, and from the great variety of audiences to which any university president must speak.

And finally, by far the majority of any president's speeches are made from notes, with no manuscript from which editorial ex-cerpts may be drawn. Sometimes these are the best and most elo-quent of all! — and the author of these chapters takes doubtful comfort in the likely illusion that he may have said better things, and said them better, than the reader of this book might suppose.

J. L. MORRILL, President
University of Minnesota

February 15, 1960

# Table of Contents

THE ONGOING STATE UNIVERSITY

# CHAPTER I

# The Land-Grant Idea

In 1962 the nation will celebrate the one hundredth anniversary of the enactment by the United States Congress of the Land-Grant Act, signed by President Abraham Lincoln. It was truly another Act of Emancipation, freeing our still-new republic from the narrowly constricted view of educational opportunity inherited from our European past. The passage of this legislation resulted in the founding or new growth of thirty-two state or territorial universities and thirty-seven other leading American colleges and technological institutes dedicated to the education and service of the American people in nearly all walks of life.

The Land-Grant Act passed in 1862 provided for the donation by the federal government of public lands "to the several states and territories which may provide colleges for the benefit of agriculture and the mechanic arts." Each state that accepted title to these lands was obligated to establish "at least one college where the leading object shall be, without excluding other scientific and classical studies, and including military tactics, to teach such branches of learning as are related to agriculture and the mechanic arts . . . in order to promote the liberal and practical education of the industrial classes in the several pursuits and professions in life."

The principle of granting land from the public domain to further the cause of education had already been established. In the

Land Ordinance of 1785, the Continental Congress reserved one lot in every township in the Northwest Territory for the maintenance of public schools, and in the Northwest Ordinance of 1787, it ruled that "the means of education shall forever be encouraged." Such encouragement could best be accomplished by land grants, for vast stretches of land were the greatest undeveloped resource of our young nation and the chief asset in the public economy.

Thus the 1862 Land-Grant Act provided that the moneys realized from the grants of land "shall constitute a perpetual fund, the capital of which shall remain forever undiminished . . . to the endowment, support, and maintenance" of the land-grant college or colleges in each state.

To understand fully the revolutionary impact of the "land-grant idea" on American higher education, we must remember the conditions of those times. During most of the nineteenth century higher education in this country was modeled on the European and the British plan. Higher education was reserved for a minority, for those students who were intended for the traditional professional careers, or for young people born into families of wealth and position who were to be trained presumably for "leadership." Most colleges were private and sectarian, and offered a strictly limited course of classical studies oriented toward the past, not toward the needs of the future and a new and growing nation. It was taken for granted that the great majority of people would be content with the rudiments of an education.

But the early American settlers and immigrants had other ideas. They were courageous and enterprising and determined to get something better for themselves and their children than their forebears in Europe had known. Their desires gave rise to the land-grant movement, which was spearheaded by farmers and rural people, especially those in the new states on the western frontier.

The University of Minnesota was one of the earliest institutions of higher education to take advantage of the provisions of the Land-Grant Act. Founded in 1851, only two years after Minnesota became a territory, eleven years before the last great Indian uprising, this university and the territory it served were typical of the pioneer spirit of the land-grant movement. It was a hard country, "a land of lonely lakes and rivers." The fierce, ice-locked winters drove many a new settler southward to a gentler climate. Fear of the Indians discouraged others. But more sturdy settlers arriving to try their luck on the rich land near Stillwater and St. Paul were jubilant at the prospects of farming.

Almost immediately, however, they faced a problem of great importance to them. How would they ever get schools in this wild country? What would happen to their children, growing up with no education and no understanding of anything but plowing and hunting and woodcutting? And so these pioneers built schoolhouses with their own hands — one-room log huts with roughhewed log benches. There was little money in the territory. Barter was the order of the day, and it took a determined schoolteacher to come out to one of those log huts and teach for a salary often consisting only of eggs and pigs and ears of corn. It took equally determined parents to scrape together enough to support a teacher.

But there were dreamers among the new citizens. These men and women, struggling to maintain the barest kind of elementary education, even dared to dream of founding a great university. And this they did. In only the second session of the territorial legislature, in 1851, the believers in publicly supported higher education in Minnesota rose to their feet and proposed — and achieved — the founding of a public center for higher learning.

In sister states, other men of like mind were joining in the demand for national support of public, practical higher education. It was the time of the triumph of Jacksonian democracy, with its new belief in the dignity and worth of each individual, and of the free school movement with its credo that education is a public obligation. Old Jonathan Turner of Illinois pleaded throughout the 1850's for a "Common Man's Educational Bill of Rights," and the plea fell on many responsive ears and hearts.

The author of the Land-Grant Act, United States Senator Justin S. Morrill of Vermont, was the son of a blacksmith and vitally interested in the "farmers and mechanics and all those who must win their bread by labor." The first Morrill Act to establish land-grant colleges was passed by Congress in 1859, but vetoed by President Buchanan. Morrill and the men who believed as he did in the vital importance of education for the common man did not give up. In 1862, during the dark early hours of the Civil War, Congress again passed Senator Morrill's land-grant bill, and this time President Lincoln signed the bill into law. Thus after a long struggle and many rebuffs, the movement to establish public industrial and agricultural colleges was successful.

The passage of the Land-Grant Act gave a financial footing and a new sense of direction and responsibility to higher education in the United States. With the further help of later legislation — particularly the Hatch Act of 1887 providing for the first federal support for research, and the Smith-Lever Act of 1914, authorizing the organization and support of an agricultural extension service conducted jointly by the federal government and the states through their land-grant institutions — the United States has today developed the most extensive system of higher and adult education in the world.

The land-grant colleges arose from a national need. They were the products of a democratic demand which the higher education of their day neither recognized nor would have been disposed to meet if it had. In the climate of then contemporary academic attitudes, they were unwelcome; and their purpose — "to promote the liberal and practical education of the industrial classes" — was poorly regarded. If they were to succeed, they must not only prove their place by service in each state, but must also gain strength as progressive partners in service to the nation.

It was a hard assignment — requiring leaders of social insight, leaders with an indomitable faith in a destiny still to be determined. One of the greatest of these leaders was Dr. William Oxley Thompson, president of the Ohio State University. He spoke with the zeal of a reformer. He urged a broadened curriculum adequate to an expanding economy, an economy dependent for its development upon science and industry. He reminded the struggling land-grant colleges of his day that they were really national universities and must meet the measure of national need and greatness.

Thompson stressed the spreading service of the land-grant institutions to the children of the common people, their strength at the grass roots of American democracy. Reasoning from the land-grant precedent of federal support, in cooperation with the states, he spelled out more than fifty years ago the completely convincing argument for federal aid to the public schools which the federal government still, incomprehensibly, lacks the courage or conviction to concede, but which is inevitable.

Practical utility, not snobbish academic respectability or any notion of intellectual aristocracy, must be the test of institutional integrity, he declared. "An institution," he said, "is to be operated for the good it can do; for the people it can serve; for the science it can promote; for the civilization it can advance." That summons needs no revision today.

The land-grant tradition which such dedicated men helped to establish has more than any other single influence shaped the pattern of higher education in America today. In all the long tradition of higher education, ancient and modern, in the Western world, the land-grant colleges and universities are unique. They have created what has been described as the most comprehensive system of scientific, technical, and practical higher education the world has ever known.

American university research was an adaptation of the German genius. Commitment to the liberal arts (with the American invention of the four-year liberal arts college) was a heritage from the medieval universities and the Renaissance, transmitted to our shores through Oxford and Cambridge. But America's needs were new and different, practical and urgently immediate to meet the requirements of an expanding democratic and economic order. They required a broader curriculum and a more democratic widening of educational opportunity.

The land-grant institutions provided not only "liberal" but "practical" education. Not only were the traditional scholastic and professional subjects retained in the combined land-grant and state universities, but workaday agriculture and the mechanic arts entered into the academic environment, gaining dignity and aca-

7

demic acceptance and the methodology of science and scholarship thereby, contributing the challenge of *useful* relevance to a concept of culture too remote from the problems of daily life and work.

These institutions brought education not only for men but equally for women; the opportunity of learning not just for a well-to-do or intellectual elite but for all who must carry the burdens of citizenship and productive service in a great and growing nation.

This has been the American answer to the question "Who shall be educated?" — as contrasted with the restrictive and highly selective philosophy of Great Britain and the Continental countries. There the opportunity for university education has been historically reserved for an elite of not more than 5 per cent — insead of our 25 per cent — of the college-age population, an elite presumably prepared to lead the masses of the peasantry, the proletariat, and an inert middle class.

The great modern state universities have outgrown, of course, the early and limited land-grant-college assignment of "agriculture and the mechanic arts." They take all knowledge for their province and have enlarged incalculably the modest beginnings of research which the federal government made possible for the land-grant institutions under the Hatch Act of 1887. The land-grant funds, so vital for the founding and growth of many state colleges and universites, provide today but a small part of the public moneys needed to operate them. It is the taxes of all the people primarily, both state and federal taxes, which now support and sustain these institutions.

In recent years the land-grant idea has met new questions about the future. Has the land-grant college or university any longer a special function — other than in agriculture? Has it still the opportunity to pioneer? Because of widespread acceptance and imitation of the land-grant idea and philosophy, have our institutions fulfilled the ancient admonition to find themselves by losing themselves? Do we have still the opportunity and the need for leadership — the land-grant leadership that historically was "unique, distinct, and indispensable"?

8

What will we do about the inevitably rising costs which will have to be met if we are to provide widespread educational opportunity for the larger numbers of American youth? Can we face up educationally through teaching and research to the incredible postwar explosion of knowledge? Is there a counter-trend, arising from these exigencies, toward enforced tuition increases in the public institutions and toward more restrictive admissions?

The idea has been expressed that, after all, "mass education" has been a mistake, and that quality and quantity in American higher education are incompatible. The notion has been revived in some quarters that the time has come for a partial retreat to the ancient academic tradition of the Ivory Tower — a notion argued more especially at the moment in the demand for secondary school reforms.

The Soviet challenge of the Sputniks and Luniks has raised the cry for more specialized and selective training in science and technology. These, to be sure, have been mainstays of the land-grant progam — but our job has always been more than that. It has been, through all these years, the mandate of the Land-Grant Act "to promote" — without excluding other scientific and *classical* studies, beyond agriculture and the mechanic arts, and including military tactics — "the *liberal* and practical education of the industrial classes in the *several* pursuits and professions of life."

That mission has been accomplished magnificently. More than half of all World War II officers for the nation's defense, for example, were commissioned through the land-grant Reserve Officers' Training Corps (the ROTC). In 1957–58 — the latest date for which I have statistics — more than 43 per cent of all doctoral degrees granted in the social sciences by all American institutions were awarded by the land-grant colleges and universities, 45 per cent of all the doctorates in English and journalism, 47 per cent of all those in the fine arts, and 38 per cent of all those in foreign languages and literature.

Far more than a third of all our land-grant college and university students are enrolled in our colleges and divisions of liberal arts and sciences, as they should be in a society with such need for skills

9

and leadership in all "the several pursuits and professions of life." The fastest-rising enrollments in most of our institutions are in science and engineering; but this country needs all kinds of educated citizens, and relies on all our colleges and universities, both public and private, to produce them. Between the periods 1926–30 and 1946–50, with a population increase of a little over 20 per cent, the numbers of bachelor's degrees granted by all the colleges and universities of the country increased from 551,000 to 1,421,000 — a leap of 158 per cent.

It was the land-grant idea that long since had opened the doors — the idea that Edmund J. James, former president of the University of Illinois, declared to be "the beginning of one of the most comprehensive, far-reaching . . . schemes for the endowment of higher education ever adopted by any civilized nation."

At the same time, no American college or university of importance and integrity, unless forced by failure of financial support, will abandon the idea of excellence or the pursuit of the first-rate in the effort to serve larger numbers. The land-grant institutions will cling to standards and strive to upgrade them.

Actually, "the true greatness of American higher education is held aloft on the two pillars of quality and quantity," as President C. W. de Kiewiet of the privately supported University of Rochester has said. Dr. de Kiewiet has further warned against any imitation by this country of the restrictive and selective practices in higher education in the European countries. The infiltration of communism in French political life, and of socialism in British liberal politics, he attributed in significant measure to the disappointment and sense of frustration among the youth of those nations, deprived of the opportunity for advanced education, without hope of finding a place in society suited to their talents.

"What is missing in those countries," President de Kiewiet said, "is the acceptance by [their] universities of a proper responsibility to help in the training of the student of good but not [exclusively] first-rate ability. . . . [The] ordinary American graduate . . . [the] run-of-mine student who would have little chance of being accepted in a British or French university, acquires a literateness in science, an awareness in political and economic issues, a receptiveness in technological affairs, that in their sum total are an incalculable national asset."

Today nations overseas are beginning to awake from their mistake, with Russia leading the way, perhaps, but with our American land-grant colleges and universities serving as a far truer beacon of the free and democratic educational way.

Former President Charles Seymour of Yale University once described the land-grant university as having won its position in the American educational scene "by reason of its sense of responsibility for the welfare of the community." This is the continuing challenge of the land-grant idea to the modern state university. Persistence in old patterns, however resourceful and valid in their day, is never sufficient for the future — the future which all too soon becomes the pressing present. Yet the goals of the land-grant movement have never lost their integrity. They require only reaffirmation and rededication in the wider and more complex contemporary context of the great state universities of today.

# CHAPTER II

# Knowledge for Use

Born of the American democratic ideal, nourished and encouraged by the passage of the Land-Grant Act in 1862, the state universities have grown and flourished all across the nation. From the beginning their philosophy emphasized not only education for all the people but also "knowledge for use." The purpose of the state university is the threefold task of teaching, research, and public service; and in each of these three duties the emphasis has been on the usefulness and relevance of all learning to a better life and to the maintenance of a free and democratic society.

Knowledge for use has not been the credo of the state universities only. More than one hundred years ago, the celebrated Cardinal Newman wrote his great book *The Idea of a University*. The Cardinal, of course, could not foresee the kind of world this would be a century ahead — or the kind of universities it would require — but his definition of a university as "a place of concourse whither students come from every quarter for every kind of knowledge" needs no revision for the great state universities of today; nor does his often-quoted statement that "if, then, a practical end must be assigned to a university course, I say it is that of training good members of society."

Doctors, lawyers, teachers, engineers, and men and women seeking nearly any other career that one could name — these the state university is organized to train in their useful skills; but this is only part of the task. The training of "good members of society," of citizens ennobled by understanding, capable of thinking sensibly and acting fairly, has always been the larger purpose of the state university.

The state universities have managed in an amazing degree to envelop and adapt the strong heritage from the British and German universities, while making room for indigenous new contributions of their own. Most notable of these has been their democratic American commitment to the land-grant ideal of educating larger numbers, of bringing the occupations of an agricultural and industrial society into the intellectual environment of the university, of serving ingeniously and usefully the community from which the sources of their strength arise.

In this commitment to knowledge for use there has been, of course, the ever-present danger of dispersion, of too superficial an answer *ad hoc,* of wasting effort upon the exigent and expedient. But the need has been greater than the risk — and who can doubt that the need is greater than ever today? Doing the things that needed to be done, becoming what it was useful and necessary to become, the state university has grown in stature, without sacrifice of the historic function of universities.

More than two decades ago, Dr. Lotus D. Coffman, my distinguished predecessor in the Minnesota presidency, spoke out for the American state university with perhaps the clearest, broadest, and most realistic definition of that institution ever phrased. He was addressing an important conference, with distinguished educators in attendance mostly from the great private universities in this country and including many from the oldest and most respected institutions overseas. His bold and uncompromising statement sounded, for those days, a startling note:

"Growing out of and flourishing in the very soil of democracy, supported and maintained by all the people, committed unequivocally to a more highly trained intelligence of the masses, believing that the road to intellectual opportunity should never be closed, maintaining a wide-open door for all those . . . willing to make the trial, the state universities, nevertheless, have held in common with the private universities a high sense of obligation with regard to the necessity of advancing human knowledge, of promoting research, and of training those of superior gifts for special leadership.

"The state universities hold that there is no intellectual service too undignified for them to perform. They maintain that every time they lift the intellectual level of any class or group, they enhance the intellectual opportunities of every class or group.

"They maintain that every time they teach any group or class the importance of relying on tested information as the basis for action, they advance the cause of science. They maintain that every time they teach any class or group in society how to live better, to read more and to read more discriminatingly, to do any of the things which stimulate intellectual or aesthetic interest and effort, they thereby enlarge the group's outlook on life, make its members more cosmopolitan in their points of view, and improve their standard of living.

"Such services as these the state universities would not shrink from performing — indeed would seek to perform."

Even though these ideals are far from fully realized, the state universities need no broader charter today. These words still express the best credo we can muster. There is room in it for our expanding American democracy, but little for the concepts that have guided the universities in ancient times, in aristocratic societies, or in totalitarian states.

The philosophy of knowledge for use has had its enemies, not only in other times and cultures but in our own democratic society. It is a cause against which the strong pressures of both past and present sometimes threaten to persuade us. The spirit of the ancient Oxford don who proclaimed that the worth of knowledge lies in the degree of its uselessness haunts us still, while from the other extreme the present-day insistence that all knowledge be immediately practical and provable is just as unrealistic.

In higher education the inertia of the cherished classical university tradition too often is a dead weight on our efforts to revitalize the liberal arts, to make them more relevant to the lives and work of the present generation. Too often, in faculty debates upon the curriculum, I have been reminded of John Dewey's caustic observation that "to set up as protector of a shrinking classicism requires only the accident of a learned education, the possession of leisure, a reasonably apt memory for some phrases and a facile pen for others." "The beginning of culture," he said, "would be to cease plaintive eulogies of a past culture, eulogies which carry only a few yards before they are drowned in the noise of the day."

Please do not mistake my meaning. As one whose undergraduate major was Latin and Greek and who hoped to become a teacher of the classics, I do not mean to depreciate the priceless heritage of the past. George Gissing's *Private Papers of Henry Ryecroft* would be among the ten books I'd like to have if marooned on a desert island.

But new occasions should teach new duties. With the philosopher Alfred North Whitehead, I deeply believe that "education is the acquisition of the art of the *utilization* of knowledge"; that essentially "culture should be for action"; that "the careful shielding of a university from the activities of the world around it is the best way to kill interest and to defeat progress"; that "celibacy does not suit a university . . . it must mate itself with action."

"Action" is the key word in that admonition. Goethe's remark that "there is nothing more frightful than ignorance in action" we have every reason in our time to remember. Pleading, indeed, the present-day usefulness of ancient thought when taught with current insight, the British classical scholar Sir Richard Livingstone was prophetic when he wrote that "an uninstructed public is a temptation and an opportunity for the liar, the charlatan and the fraud." We do not forget, either, the warning of Thomas Jefferson, whose own proudest achievement was his establishment of the University of Virginia, that "if a nation expects to be both ignorant and free, it expects what never was and never will be."

Carved in stone on the Minnesota campus is the affirmation that the university was "founded in the faith that men are ennobled by understanding." This, too, is the mandate of knowledge for use.

Education is useful, as Whitehead also said, because understanding is useful.

This is the heart of the matter: the idea that the citizens of a democracy need knowledge; that learning is more than an ornament; and that instruction must be useful. Yet despite the testimony of so many democrats and scholars, the common sense of "knowledge for use" is never quite conceded, as we all well know, in the unending debate and dialectic of higher education.

The competing claims of liberal versus vocational education, of "culture versus cash," of secularism versus humanism, of science versus the humanities, the elective system versus the closed curriculum — these have been the controversies of the last one hundred and fifty years in American higher education on the battleground more often of semantics than common sense. Meanwhile knowledge has so multiplied, society and the education which serves it have become so specialized, that the old question of "what knowledge is of most worth" must go unanswered even among the philosophers.

Inevitably, I think, we are driven to the criterion of usefulness — and in higher education, despite the debates that never will be stilled, America has chosen that standard for advance. What a nation needs is the final determinant of what it will expect its institutions to accomplish and will support them in achieving. To the whole tradition of higher education in the Western world, dating back to medieval times, America has made one major contribution — the democratization of educational opportunity at the higher levels, responding to the not-to-be denied demand of knowledge for use.

The American university today is the historical product of three major streams of influence, it seems to me — two of these from other lands and times, only one strictly indigenous and native to the American need and dream.

The first of these streams of influence was the British one, coming to the colonial college from Oxford and Cambridge, linked with the intellectual tradition of the great Continental universities of the twelfth to the fourteenth centuries, Paris and Bologna, Salerno, and others. Here the learned professions were born. Here was the domain of the trivium and quadrivium, of the dialecticians deep in argument, of the religio-humanistic ideal of the "Christian gentleman" so richly nourished by the New England college of the 1880's. This heritage endures today in the liberal arts commitment of our colleges and universities.

The second great stream of influence was that of the pre-World War I German university with its impersonal zeal for scholarship per se, its introduction of the laboratory and the seminar, its relentless pursuit of research and scientific experimentation in the climate of freedom to learn and to teach.

These ideals, springing from the renaissance of the German national state, were transfused into the American higher educational bloodstream by the multitude of American students and scholars who had poured into the German universities, led by Edward Everett who took his Doctor of Philosophy degree from Göttingen in 1819, the first American to be awarded that degree. These Americans came back to positions of leadership in American colleges and universities. The fruits of their zeal persist strongly in the present-day American university.

The third great influence has been that of the American state university — especially the land-grant state university, made possible by the Morrill Act of 1862. This great scheme of federal-state cooperation, dedicated to "liberal and practical education," not only opened the doors of educational opportunity to American youth, but also brought science to the study of agriculture and to every realm of teaching and research. It was an act directly aimed at knowledge for use and social action.

Infused by all three influences is the typical American university today, whether public or private. But in the state university, above all, the determining force of educational development has been the democratic idea of the wider utilization of knowledge for individual growth and social advance.

In England in recent years there have been new stirrings toward these same objectives; but European education, as former President Arthur E. Morgan of Antioch College observed, "continues the old tradition of preparing small groups of educated intellectuals to lead a relatively inert mass."

"America," he said, "has larger hopes. It is endeavoring somewhat blindly to explore the whole range of human capacities, to discover what can be added to the life of every person to give it the greatest range, satisfaction and value. . . . Limited objectives like those of Europe can more quickly bring excellence, but the American ideal finally will achieve greater dignity and range."

The land-grant philosophy has been America's most fundamental contribution to higher education, but there have been two other significant movements and reforms in American universities and colleges since colonial days — the victory of the elective system, and the more recent trend toward "general education." Each of them has been a determined assault upon the strongholds of academic tradition. Each has been a militant protest against the academic status quo, reflecting the surge of transcendent social needs and forces against the campus gates. Each has been an urgent effort to serve better the aim of knowledge for use.

The offering of elective courses rather than a prescribed and unvarying classical curriculum is today taken for granted in the liberal arts colleges of the state universities and in most private colleges. In its extreme form, it has been justifiably criticized as "bargain-counter education," and it did indeed release forces of undisciplined reaction that went too far. But the elective system was indispensable to the emancipation of the higher education of its time.

In the second of these American innovations — the growth of "general education" — there has been a conscious effort to provide, through education, the common basis for both living and working in a free society. There has been also the enormously hopeful and significant determination to establish definitive educational objectives, based on research; to remake instruction in terms of those objectives; and to demand the proof of results through scientific evaluation.

This trend has been part of a changing outlook toward the

objectives and outcomes of liberal education, a fairly recent change in which the celebrated Harvard Report on *General Education in a Free Society* and the emphasis on "general education" in the report of the President's Commission on Higher Education are significant portents. There have been distinguished and sincere critics of the educational philosophy expressed in both documents; but there is a growing acceptance in the American academic world, I think, of the Harvard concession that generalized and specialized education are two halves of a whole, that the two must somehow be combined and given to all students alike, and finally, that knowledge must be made more viable, learning more useful and functional.

The ancient dichotomy of "liberal" versus "vocational" education will eventually be dissolved, it seems to me, because any definition of education for citizenship must take account both of living and working. This means, of course, that no narrowly intensive preoccupation with mere vocational utility will suffice. It is from the humanistic and social studies and from religious inspiration that the judgments of value come and the ethical guidance of action. In our large state universities, indeed, there is the uneasy awareness that specialized training alone is not sufficient unto the day and may be, in fact, the evil thereof.

But the complexities of modern life require more specialization, not less. Career education is, understandably, the central concern of the modern undergraduate, especially in the state universities. Youth needs motivation, but young people can and do learn, brilliantly and substantially, when educational objectives are so defined as to become intelligible and exciting personal objectives. General education is the effort to make learning more relevant to life.

The problem of present-day undergraduate education, then, is not that it is over-professionalized but that it is under-liberalized. The newer task confronting liberal education is to take full advantage of career motivation, and to permeate professional and vocational education with historical and social perspective, and with ethical meaning and orientation. Surely nothing less can stand sufficient in a democracy whose present and future citizens, as Sir Norman Angell put it, "must manage civilization in their spare time." Every citizen participates in the shaping of social policy, whether he knows it or not. His enlightenment is thus an urgent public concern, for the price of his ignorance may be the destruction of the community.

Closely related to the need for education for citizenship and knowledge for use is the very special commitment of the land-grant state universities to the national welfare and the national defense. These universities are obligated by the terms of the Morrill Act to offer military training to their men students. This historic obligation, moral as well as legal, is definite — although not so well understood by all our students and faculty in recent years as it should have been.

In wartime, colleges and universities the country over are called on for training — the general training of top-grade young people capable of contributing to the national welfare in a hundred different fields, and the specialized training of selected students for special duty in the armed forces. In World War II, the state universities came to be mainly campuses of marching men and uniformed women, in training for the Army, Navy, Air Force, and nursing services. The larger state universities also become the arsenals of special research — "basic and fundamental," such as the development of atomic energy, and "applied," in such fields as electronics, biological and medical investigation, and guided missiles.

In the period immediately following World War II the state universities, along with all the private colleges, faced another serious problem related to their wartime service — the task of accommodating thousands of veterans seeking higher education under the GI Bill of Rights. The federal payments to the colleges and universities under this bill fell far short of meeting the additional costs of this vast influx of new students — just as the moderate tuition fees of state universities today do not begin to cover the cost of student instruction. Yet it had been the land-grant dream that no student who could profit from a college education should be turned away — and with sacrifice and struggle, with overcrowding and understaffing, the problems of the "veterans' bulge" were somehow met and overcome.

Civilian defense, it now appears, will make new demands in the future upon the state universities which are equipped with staff and facilities to deal with problems of radioactivity, biological warfare, public health and sanitation, and public utilities. Language training, geographical and anthropological knowledge, political and psychological expertness — all these and other skills taught by the state universities and other colleges become vitally important in meeting the needs of national mobilization. Here, too — in the special and urgent context of war, as well as in learning's natural climate of peace — the state university is deeply committed to knowledge for use.

During the past twenty or twenty-five years, the proportion of college-age young people in the colleges and universities of this country has increased one per cent a year, on the average. How has this come about, and what has it meant? A statement issued a few years ago by the Association of American Universities sums up our educational history:

"For 300 years higher education has played a leading role in the advancement of American civilization. No country in history so early perceived the importance of that role, and none has derived such wide-spread benefits from it . . .

"Today our universities are the standard-bearers of our whole system of education. They are the prime source of our competence in science and the arts. They are the mainstays of the professions. The names of their graduates crowd the honor rolls of two world wars and of the nation's peacetime affairs. These universities have supplied intellectual capital as essential to our society as financial capital is to our industrial enterprise. . . .

"In the United States there is a greater degree of educational equality of opportunity than anywhere else in the world. A larger proportion of Americans study in universities and colleges than any other people. These universities have more than justified the faith of the public in our distinctive system of higher education. They have proved themselves dynamic forces of American progress."

In this shining record the state universities have had a large, perhaps a major part. They have demonstrated the capacity to take new directions, to make conscious and inventive responses to new conditions without losing their sense of the historic mission of universities. That historic mission is still to be the "thinking devices of society," to work with ideas — to transmit and reinterpret the ideas that have stood the test of time, to create and discover new ones, to refine and polish them on the flint surfaces of other minds, and to put ideas to the use and inspiration of humankind.

The state university is, and must be, a composite of highly individual attitudes and judgments arrived at in different ways, by differing intellectual approaches, indeed sometimes inconsistent, but all in the environment of intellectual freedom. It encourages the free competition and the exacting appraisal of ideas. It abhors conformity and authoritarian regimentation and kindles devotion to the great codes of science and scholarship and the search for truth.

The fruits of scholarship are offered by the state university as knowledge for use — and not only knowledge but "arts and habits," as the English poet William Cory wrote a century ago. You go to a great school, he said, "for the habit of attention, for the art of expression, for the art of assuming at a moment's notice a new intellectual position, for the art of entering quickly into another person's thoughts, for the habit of submitting to censure and refutation, for the art of indicating assent or dissent in graduated terms, for the habit of regarding minute points of accuracy, for the art of working out what is possible in a given time — for taste, for discrimination, for mental courage and mental soberness."

All these arts and habits of scholarship and the useful knowledge they produce are the central business of the state university. There is no one in our society today who has not benefited in countless ways from the dissemination of these arts and habits and their useful products. The skillful doctor in his diagnoses, the educated

mother in the upbringing of her children, the trained social work-
er at work upon community problems, the learned judge upon the
bench, the conscientious legislator serving in committee — all these
and myriad others, directly or indirectly, have reason to depend in
the modern world upon the attitudes and methods of scholarship
and the fruits thereof learned in the state universities and put to
ever-increasing use.

# CHAPTER III

# Servant to All the People

THE great universities of today grew in size and service as the population expanded and the needs and aspirations of the American people multiplied. The threefold commitment of the land-grant state university — to teaching, to research, and to public service — has been defined more and more clearly through the years, both through federal legislation (with the Land-Grant Act, the Hatch Act of 1887, and the Smith-Lever Act of 1914) and state legislation, but most of all through the demands and ambitions of the people of each state.

Each of the land-grant state universities is committed to the belief that its true campus covers the entire state it serves. Further than this, each has recognized that knowledge transcends both state and national boundaries, and that a state university dedicated only to the narrow needs of its own state would prove too limited in its vision to meet even those needs adequately. The modern state university serves its own state best through its work in the wider world of science and scholarship with students, teachers, and researchers from every state and nation.

In a state university the public interest must be paramount. In Minnesota, we set great store by the constitutional status of our university and the independence it thereby enjoys. However, these came first from the people, and we can presume too much upon

24

them. Such autonomy is vital as a time-giving protection against the changing winds of partisan politics and shortsighted prejudice, which sometimes blow in fitful gusts. But the university is not superior to the state. It is the servant of the state. Its dimensions are determined by the extent of public interest and support. Its destiny as an institution "of . . . and from the people" is the product of public understanding — understanding of its heritage in the whole tradition of universities in the Western world, far older than this nation or any state, but revitalized in the American milieu; understanding of its impartial but imperative usefulness to the individual and society, of its creative resourcefulness as "the developmental arm of the state," in the phrase of the late President David Kinley of Illinois.

Here is taxation *with* representation. This is important: that the tax-contributed millions invested annually by state appropriations in the ongoing of the state university should yield real and realizable dividends — young men and women who will be more capable in their careers and their communities by reason of their training here and better citizens by reason of a broader understanding.

The state university is many things to many people. To some, of course, special training for a job is the all-important objective — very often just a better paid and more interesting job than any to which they could attain without low-cost college education or professional training. But others see the university in terms of its research and public services — better farming through agricultural research carried into rural life by university extension work; better health through better trained doctors, up-to-the-minute in their knowledge of medical investigation and discovery; larger payrolls and profits through industrial and business research. These purposes and scores more, all of them different, the university is expected to serve.

The state university is representative of dynamic American democracy beyond the obligation of providing educational opportunity for youth, and beyond the public services that the citizens of the state increasingly demand of it in their insistent appeals to the faculty, the trustees and administration, and the state legislature. It is representative in its zeal for exploration and discovery. Research is that which activates the university enterprise, which inspires instruction and the urgent commitment of its staff to public service. The laboratories and libraries, the hospitals and engineering shops of the large state universities, are the workshops of creative and inventive minds. Only this wide-ranging and productive use could justify their cost. Cancer that kills and the vast variety of other human ills, the secrets of nuclear power which mankind is only beginning to understand, the never-solved problems of plant and animal production, the discovery and development of human and natural resources — challenges like these are the fundamental business of the state university.

The services of the modern state university can be better understood, perhaps, if we consider one typical land-grant university and its relation to its state. The University of Minnesota, the institution I know best, is larger than many state universities, not so large as others, but representative in most ways of the land-grant idea and the state university philosophy. Recognized as one of the great universities of the nation, a leader in scholarship and research, the University of Minnesota is more than an institution — it is a dynamic force.

In February 1851, however, when the University of Minnesota was chartered by the territorial legislature, the eminence it was to attain could hardly have been envisioned. It seems strange today that those hard-pressed pioneers should have given thought to a university at a time when the wilderness was just beyond the barn and the first clump of trees. Yet by November 1851, a preparatory school was opened with a teacher and twenty students, and in 1856 construction was begun on Old Main — a three-story, white stone building with accommodations for several hundred students — the first home of the university.

As so often happened in those early, bravely optimistic days, the plans for a great university far outstripped the immediate resources of the people. In 1857 came a depression, and in 1861 the

26

Civil War. A half mile from the bank of the Mississippi River, Old Main lay half-finished and deserted, except for a caretaker who, with his family and a flock of turkeys, inhabited the first floor. But war and depression were not enough to deflect the frontier people from their dreams of higher education. In 1869 the first freshman class of the reorganized University of Minnesota — eighteen students in all — took their places in that first building which had now been finished, symbolizing the secure establishment of the university.

Old Main is no more. It was destroyed by fire in 1904, and another building now stands in its place. Beside that building there are others, great aisles of buildings, extending along the river bank for over a mile. As the state has grown in numbers and in needs, so has the university. Today the campus is almost literally state-wide, with its more than one hundred major buildings on the main campus in Minneapolis, some 112 buildings on the 726 acres of the agricultural campus in St. Paul, a splendid branch in Duluth, and its schools of agriculture and experiment stations in many parts of the state.

More than 36,000 individual full-time students were enrolled at Minnesota over the three quarters of the academic year 1958–59, but this is only a fraction of the total number taught. In that same year, for example, more than 87,000 people were actually enrolled in the organized instructional program of the university in correspondence study, extension classes, short courses, professional institutes, and the like. Through the agricultural extension service, including the work of county agents and 4-H Club workers, more than 178,000 farm families were given assistance and instruction by the university.

Thus, up in the Red River Valley, a group of 4-H Club youth prepare for a state agricultural contest with the help of a university extension agent. In St. Paul the members of labor unions study the possibilities for workers' education in evening extension courses. In a southern Minnesota community, farm housewives counsel with a university home demonstration agent on how to improve the everyday conditions of rural life. On the Minneapolis campus the Municipal Reference Bureau provides research and informational services for 400 Minnesota communities. The Industrial Relations Center offers research and training activities designed to serve both employers and employees, management and labor leaders. At Grand Rapids a short course is offered for summer resort operators and workers. In widely scattered public schools children hear special programs broadcast from the campus.

The listening and learning audience of the university radio station is estimated at two million people, "sitting in" on convocations and even classroom lectures, hearing good music, sharing information and inspiration in many fields. Educational television programs produced and sponsored by the university reach many in the metropolitan areas. Through its organized concert, lecture, and school assembly services, more than a million and a half people hear musicians, artists, and lecturers sponsored by the university.

In the short courses and institutes conducted on the St. Paul and Minneapolis campuses, thousands from every community of the commonwealth — including men and women highly trained professionally but seeking to keep abreast of new knowledge — share their experiences and draw upon university science and scholarship for the solution of new problems. Week after week, new groups come to the Continuation Study Center on the Minneapolis campus to learn about atomic power and its control, accounting, housing, sanitary engineering, employment office operation, the management of cooperatives — the list of subjects is as long as the inventory of things people must understand and must do.

Education is thus sent out and diffused through the whole state, as the pioneers hoped and intended. Here is knowledge in use in the adult arena of daily social and civic imperatives. Broadly chartered and broadly intentioned, the university extends its reach in the directions of need.

Yet in Minnesota, as elsewhere, the state university's open invitation to all to study and learn has been no commitment to mediocrity. When President Coffman spoke of the door to intellectual opportunity which should never be closed, the key word of his concept was "intellectual." The pursuit of excellence has been intrinsic in the mission of our academic community — and at the University of Minnesota the too current dichotomy of quality versus quantity has been proven false. Size, it has been demonstrated, need be no handicap to excellence.

The University of Minnesota was a pioneer in the statewide testing of high-school students, and one of the first in the nation to include aptitude testing in its admission procedures. Few universities can point to so complete a record of constant self-examination and experimentation to screen qualifications, to identify ability, and to adjust instructional techniques to develop it. Enrolling approximately half of all the college students in Minnesota, the university retains the distinction of having the highest average and the highest range of college aptitude test scores in its College of Science, Literature, and the Arts for entering freshmen in any type of college in the state. In the Institute of Technology the student ability potential is even higher. The Law School has lately modified completely its admission requirements in order to ensure still higher professional standards. Yet in keeping with the land-grant philosophy of education for all and the need for general as well as specialized education, the university in its General College offers admission to any Minnesota high school graduate and the opportunity to try out determination and capacity to succeed.

Size has *not* negated quality. It has fortified our competence to attain excellence by enlarging the range of opportunity to discover and develop human ability — and to encourage and incite each student to his highest possible level of intellectual endeavor and performance.

I have mentioned only a few of the many divisions, departments, and colleges that carry on the first part of the state university's threefold task — teaching. More nearly than Ezra Cornell could have hoped, state universities today are institutions in which almost "any person can find instruction in almost any study." At the University of Minnesota undergraduate and graduate courses are offered in all the arts and sciences and nearly every other field of knowledge—from the engineering of a farm tractor to the study of nuclear potentials; from insect extermination to the classical philosophers; from anthropology to zoology—literally, from A to Z.

Most closely and especially concerned with the teaching function in all its aspects is the College of Education. The University of Minnesota has long recognized that "the eggs of education are all in one basket," so to say, and that the opportunities of higher education are part of a continuum which begins in the kindergarten and the first grade. In this partnership the university and the public schools stand together, interdependent, the university relying upon the elementary and high schools for the preparation of its students, and the public schools looking to the university and other colleges for the training of teachers and for educational research.

"The whole history of education," Jonathan Turner said in 1850, "shows that we must begin with the higher institutions or we can never succeed with the lower; for the plain reason that neither knowledge nor water can run uphill." But neither can the higher institutions succeed without the lower. The public schools are the indispensable testing ground of educational advance.

The University of Minnesota and its College of Education serve the public schools and people of the state, not only through teacher training — including the maintenance of university nursery, elementary, and high schools for practice teaching — but also through measurement, guidance, and curriculum studies, through provision of public health and hygiene resources, through educational and advisory services for schoolmen and local government personnel alike, through arrangement of school assembly programs, through audiovisual and teacher placement services, through institutes and short courses and summer session classes.

The College of Agriculture and the Institute of Technology are also two main foundation-stones of the University of Minnesota, in keeping with the original emphasis in the Land-Grant Act on "agriculture and the mechanic arts." In these fields, as in so many others, the teaching function is inseparably related to research. Teaching and experimentation go on together at every level in forestry and animal husbandry; in our School of Veterinary Medicine, newly established in direct response to the demands of the agricultural people of Minnesota; in our Mines Experiment Station devoted to the problems of iron ore; in the hydraulics laboratory beside the Mississippi River; in all branches of engineering and architecture, home economics and plant pathology.

In the Graduate School especially, and in the Medical School, teaching and research become still more indistinguishable. Postgraduate training in the professions and in the specialized fields of knowledge, with the granting of advanced degrees, is one of the university's major functions. At the University of Minnesota graduate study is carried on in more than a hundred fields of knowledge, and the graduate enrollment is the third largest in the university.

In all the subject-matter disciplines, in science, and in training for the professions, teaching goes forward through research. The nationwide pre-eminence of the University of Minnesota Medical School offers an example. The training of physicians and surgeons, once the function of proprietary schools, was revitalized when transferred to the university environment under the stimulus and the corrective of basic investigation in the medical and biological sciences. This has been true everywhere, but the alliance of the University of Minnesota with the distinguished achievements of the Doctors Mayo through the Mayo Foundation was epochal. It set new standards of professional training and made higher demands for professional competence. These reacted to set new goals for scholarly investigation, and the result has been a medical school of the highest stature.

Through research — the second element of our threefold purpose — a university lifts itself by its bootstraps. Its productiveness goes up; its maturity and prestige are enhanced. The interaction of school and society, at the level of research, is a chain reaction, releasing endless energy: cultural, social, and economic. To underwrite the productive ongoing of the state university is the surest investment the people of a state can make in their own future. The future of the university must be a changing one if it is to be a greater one, and research is the tested instrument of change and advance.

Research has brought the University of Minnesota world leadership in heart surgery, on the Minneapolis campus and at the affiliated Mayo Clinic at Rochester; the pioneer work of university surgeons and basic scientists and the unique Variety Club Heart Hospital are known throughout the medical world. Research has brought the rescue of a depleting iron ore industry and its renaissance in the Minnesota and national economy through the work on taconite, a low-grade iron ore, by a Minnesota professor. World-recognized leadership has been attained at the University of Minnesota in the study and control of brucellosis, a destructive disease of men and animals alike; in the biology of human starvation and the effect of diet upon cardiovascular disease; in the study of plant diseases, and of nuclear and cosmic ray and chemical phenomena.

Just as teaching and research are interdependent functions, so is the third major function of the university — public service — dependent on the other two. For the state university, service, like charity, logically begins where we live and have our being. Into the community the institution pours its flow of young people, keen and competent for the work of the day, sustaining and strengthening the resources of good citizenship. Business and industry, agriculture, government, and almost every other form of organized social activity have turned increasingly to universities, and especially the state universities, for the assistance which only their high degree of specialization can give.

As is fitting in a land grant state university, service to agriculture has been one of the most important concerns of the University of Minnesota. University experts — the county agent, the soils technician, the pasture renovator, the timber man, the drainage specialist, all part of the Agricultural Extension Division — go on, day after day, helping the farmers of the state to make the best use of agricultural advances.

Behind the county agent, behind the extension specialists, stand other men — the researchers. Much of the university's service to the state can be traced back to quiet men working in laboratories. The

work is carried on in experimental plots, in test tubes, in calcu-
lating machines, and in the complicated processes of the human
mind. In recent years it has required ever more and better teachers
and researchers, higher level and most costly training and tools.

In agriculture it is easy to see that this is indeed a good investment.

Through agricultural research, farmers achieved 37 per cent
more production per acre in the decade 1940 to 1950, and 79 per
cent more production per hour worked. University of Minnesota
research led the fight against wheat rust and the corn borer; developed the Northern Spy and Haralson apples, the Latham
raspberry, and countless other crop varieties adapted to our northern climate and soils; produced the No. 1 and No. 2 Minnesota
hogs; pioneered in the dry-lot feeding of beef cattle, in increased
dairy and poultry production, and in many more projects.

Clearly it is not possible to catalogue all the avenues and points
of service to society either of all state universities or even of one
such university. Not only in agriculture but in social work and
nursing training and research, through legal and pharmaceutical
investigation and professional preparation, from one area after another in our complex university enterprise the fruits of education
flow out into the state, the region, and the nation.

How can we possibly calculate the full value of the state university's service to the people of the state? What kind of return does
the university pay, in terms of profits, on the investment of many
millions of dollars over the years by the state's taxpayers? Much
of the profit, of course, cannot be measured by any dollars-and-cents
yardstick. What price can we place on the life of a child saved by
new techniques of heart surgery developed by university research,
or on the very real chance that university experimental work may
lead to the successful control of heart disease and cancer?

How, for example, do you measure the inspiration and competence which a young graduate of the state university has received
from his studies? How can we estimate his increased ability to enjoy life, the widening of his interests, the sharpening of his critical
and creative faculties? We must content ourselves with listing

these as intangible—but very real—profits on the investment, much as "good will" is considered an asset in any business.

But there are many aspects of the state university's work in which profits *can* be computed in terms of dollars and cents. These are found in all of the three broad areas of the university's work—in teaching, in research, in service.

Several research groups have compiled statistics estimating the value in dollars and cents of a college degree. These show that in terms of earning power, the college man has an advantage all through his earning life over the non-college man. During middle age the income of the non-college man tends to fall off, while that of the college man continues to increase into late middle age.

Individual return of this kind is one matter. But there is another, broader, area of return on the investment in state university teaching. Some 200,000 men and women, former students and graduates of the University of Minnesota, are now living in Minnesota—representing hundreds of skills that have been built into our population. Those skills largely determine our standard of living as a society. How much is it worth to have chemists, attorneys, dentists, teachers, doctors, engineers, veterinarians—not to mention farmers, businessmen, accountants, social workers, nurses—to have their skills and training ready for immediate use to serve all the rest of the state's people? Not only in terms of intangibles, but in terms of dollars kept in or added to the state's economy, the profit is immense.

In research and service the dollar investments are somewhat more measurable, and the returns more direct and, perhaps, more dramatic. Here, too, more often than not, private and federal funds come to the university to match those made available by the state. For example, the core of the construction funds for the magnificent Mayo Memorial addition to the University of Minnesota Hospitals was furnished by generous appropriations from the Minnesota state legislature—58 per cent of the total. But federal funds to the amount of 16 per cent and private funds amounting to 26 per cent of the total also went into the construction of the Memorial.

This could be called a "snowball" operation. Investment of state funds in a project frequently draws additional private and federal funds to the state. In a recent ten-year period, funds have come to the University of Minnesota from non-legislative sources for medical teaching and research amounting to almost $12 million. This money was invested in the university because the taxpayers of Minnesota had seen fit to build and support a medical school of the first rank.

Looking at the over-all annual operating costs, while the Minnesota taxpayer provided more than 38 per cent of the university's operating budget in one typical recent year, 17.5 per cent of the total operations were paid for by trust funds, gifts, and federal funds. To translate this into dollars and cents, our records show that the university spent nearly $5 million that year for research from funds other than legislative appropriations. It is interesting to note that the bulk of this money, none of it from Minnesota taxes, went for salaries — salaries which were spent in Minnesota in support of the general economy, just as are the salaries from any local industry.

The investment of legislative and federal and private funds for state university research has been considerable, but the returns have been tremendous. One University of Minnesota research project alone — the development of a method to process taconite iron ore — will yield very large dividends in the time to come. Not all research projects, of course, pay off so plainly. Some do not pay off at all; but in such cases at least we have learned what not to do. And what not to do is scientifically significant — and important in terms of cost too.

A true success story is that of the Latham raspberry developed by University of Minnesota researchers to withstand a cold climate. It has proved so profitable that it has spread across the country to become the leading American variety. Yet the Latham is only one of more than sixty different fruit varieties developed at the Excelsior Experiment Station at a total cost, over the forty-three years of the station's existence, of some $482,000. How much income has that tax money produced? Just the Latham raspberry has brought a $25 million income to Minnesota growers and nurserymen! Even without adding the income from other university-developed fruits, the return on the Minnesota tax dollar from university fruit experimentation has been well over fifty-to-one.

The story of University of Minnesota research on taconite, mentioned earlier, is perhaps the best known and most spectacular example of profitable scholarship. After many years of experimental work on ways of processing the low-grade taconite iron ore, a practical and low-cost method was developed for extracting and "pelleting" the iron minerals from the taconite. Today a billion-dollar taconite industry is in prospect for Minnesota to supplement the mining of the high-grade iron ores, now nearly exhausted.

The point of these examples is this: no university project of research and service is developed in a vacuum. The germination of any research project "seed" depends, of course, on the funds for its support. Just as we need a fertile and well-organized farm in order to produce a good field crop, we need a well-staffed and well-organized university to produce valuable research and services. Only to such a university — with its specialists in many allied fields, with its long experience in cooperative research — can scholars and scientists of the first rank be attracted. And only such men and women are capable of conceiving and carrying through the painstaking, often brilliant research projects from which we all profit.

But it takes more than the seed and seedbed to grow a crop. It takes a favorable climate. The state university, too, exists within a climate — the "climate of public opinion," a marvelously descriptive phrase. For without a friendly citizen-constituency, without its active support and cooperation, the state university simply cannot do its job. Most major research projects require legislative support over a long period of years, and often the active cooperation of individual citizens throughout the state. They need the support of members of other state governmental departments, if laboratory results are to be transformed into a concrete, effective program of service. And they need the public understanding that long-range, theoretical research is just as important as applied research, more so indeed, for without new theories and ideas today there can be no practical progress in the future.

The people of Minnesota, I am convinced, have a great pride and sense of proprietorship in their state university. They have given it a mandate for leadership — in the state, in the Upper Midwest, and in the nation. In this the University of Minnesota is typical of many great state universities, dedicated to the highest standards of scholarship and service.

Research and technology of the kind developed by the great universities have made possible for America the world's highest standard of living — and they have done this for the many, as opposed to the few. It is no accident that this revolutionary concept of the "good life" for the masses of people has been realized in a time following the introduction of the revolutionary concept of unlimited educational opportunity for all the people, not just the privileged few.

But having built the greatness of the state university, no state can take its greatness for granted. Greatness is as difficult to retain as to attain. The ever-increasing demands for knowledge — for practical, useful information — and for services of all kinds seem always to outrun the state university's ability to meet those demands.

No institution dedicated to the public good can remain static and unchanging in the face of ever-mounting needs and an ever-increasing population. Each year there will be more young men and women to teach, new and old problems for research to tackle, more Americans and more of mankind everywhere to feed, clothe, and house, and to aid toward independence, freedom, and a better life. As Anson Bartlett wrote many years ago, "Unless we carefully read the signs of the times and plant ourselves in fact, on advance ground, we will soon be left behind in the race of life."

# CHAPTER IV

# The Establishment and Administration of American Universities

THE great number of American colleges and universities, including the state universities, as well as their diversity and independence, has often confounded and been disapproved by foreign observers of the American educational scene. Indeed there has been considerable wonderment and skepticism among our academic colleagues overseas as to the standards of higher education as a whole in the United States. A recent British educational subcommittee, for example, remarked justifiably upon the absence of any centralized control of education in our country with the comment that the wide variety of colleges and universities lead "to a great disparity in the standards of education obtainable in the different institutions."

Although both Canada (except for the French-language universities) and the United States derived their heritage of higher learning essentially from the British universities at the outset, their respective policies for the establishment of new universities represent a marked departure from the British precedents. Both nations early responded to the indigenous educational demands and philosophy of fast-growing frontier societies and populations. In the United States especially, higher educational opportunity for youth

38

came more and more to be regarded as an inherent right and as a basic requirement for national progress and prosperity.

It is almost an axiom of sociological and historical research that a society is well appraised by the study of its institutions. Sir Charles G. Robertson, writing in 1930 of British universities, observed that "progressive universities are an index to a progressive society, stabilized universities to a stabilized society, and stagnant or decrepit ones to a stagnant or decrepit society." A renowned former president of Harvard University, Charles W. Eliot, wrote that "its institutions of education characterize a people as well as, or better than, any other group of its institutions."

The greater freedom to create new colleges and universities in America is an instance in point. The urge for educational opportunity at every level was at the heart of the historic American dream of freedom and democracy. Undeterred by centralized control or by such ancient and eminent precedents as Oxford and Cambridge, for example, or the later development of the University of London procedures, the American people have created a plethora of institutions — with a vastly greater proportion of college-age youth in attendance than in the British and Continental countries, and with a great heterogeneity of curricula and standards.

The Commission on Financing Higher Education, sponsored by the definitely discriminative Association of American Universities, commented upon the United States higher educational scene, at about the same time as the British committee I quoted earlier. But it took a different account of our situation. "What most protects freedom of choice in America is the great diversity of its institutions, none of which possesses over-riding power," the commission said, observing that "human beings and their institutions being what they are, total power is not safe in the hands of any single group no matter how well-intentioned."

Dr. D. W. Logan, the distinguished principal of the University of London, in an illuminating account of the historic and currently evolving British university system and the significant contribution made by his university to its development, has observed with insight that "today, in all parts of the world, there is a widespread demand for an expansion of the facilities for higher education which can be satisfied only by the creation of new universities."

In the United States this need was anticipated almost a century ago upon a pattern which essentially still persists. As in Britain and Canada, both church and state were the early progenitors of universities. In the United States, for example, there are currently 739 colleges and universities established and sponsored by religious denominations. The origin of Harvard, our oldest university, was both religious and civic — and its bold action in declaring its right to confer degrees (from 1642 onward) set a precedent followed by most of the other colonial colleges, some of which — Dartmouth and William and Mary, for example — were established by royal charter. But after the American Revolution most new colleges derived their charters from the various state governments, as all new colleges do today under requirements set down in the state constitutions or by acts of the various state legislatures.

For the establishment of new publicly supported and controlled institutions, decisions by the various state legislatures are individually required (with the exception that in some states new "junior colleges" or so-called "community colleges" with terminal two-year curricula may be created by joint action of the state board of education and the local community). But local ambitions and state legislative "logrolling" make these decisions fairly easy in most states, especially just now in response to the rising college-age population.

For the establishment of privately supported and controlled institutions, the procedure is even easier. Generally speaking, they are organized under state statutes providing for the creation of "nonprofit corporations." As such, they enjoy a large measure of exemption from local, state, and federal taxation. There is the requirement, however, in many states that a certificate of approval to conduct post-secondary education and to grant degrees must be obtained from the state superintendent of public instruction before the state will issue a charter.

Such charters are rarely denied to religious denominations and other incorporators of good and responsible repute, with the result that almost "anyone with a good idea, some support and a lot of courage can start a new college," as former President Lewis Webster Jones of Rutgers University has remarked.

So it is, in the United States, that the nine colonial colleges established before the American Revolution were added to in number and variety to the sum of 182 by the time of the American Civil War in the 1860's and to the present total of nearly 1,900. Of these, only 141 are classified as "universities." Nearly 500 are two-year junior colleges, the remainder being four-year liberal arts colleges, teachers colleges, and other professional and technological schools independent of the universities.

The distinguished President Daniel Gilman, who perhaps more than any other man gave meaning and integrity to the concept of the true university in America in his leadership and insistence upon high standards at Johns Hopkins, took note in his volume on *University Problems* in 1898 of what must seem to a foreign observer an unsystemized diversity of organization, administration, support, and program. It is the result, he said, of dedication to the fundamental principle of local self-government and of American freedom from political and ecclesiastical control. "If our universities were suffering from excessive spontaneity," he wrote, "they were at least free from extreme forms of intellectual despotism."

There are various advantages and disadvantages stemming from the American freedom of public and private agencies to establish new colleges and universities. Among the advantages are the ability of reasonably autonomous institutional faculties and governing boards to develop their own programs, and the freedom of these institutions to define and maintain academic standards appropriate to their special needs and objectives. Hundreds of different centers of academic initiative and planning are thus generated, providing a stimulus to creative program improvement and resourceful staff development. Strong "grass roots" to nourish the educational enterprise are cultivated, with people in the local community or regional area becoming interested and closely identified with the program of their own local institution.

The more than 20,000 American citizens, for example, who serve on college and university boards of control as regents or trustees have contributed immeasurably to the interpretation and support of higher education, explaining significantly the phenomenal growth of the American system. In a nation with hundreds of colleges and universities, there is likely to be a heightened sensitivity and response to local and social needs.

In England also the value of county feeling and county ties in higher education is coming to be recognized, as indicated by the statement of Sir Walter Moberly that "there is a place for idiosyncrasies redolent of particular classes, callings and localities, for a diversity of cultures enriching one another, and so perhaps for a special concern of a particular university or college with a particular region." The origin and growing influence of some of the British civic universities testify further to this thought.

More than this, the impact of universities upon their communities is a cultural and civilizing one which multiple centers of institutional influence tend to extend. This is discernible, I think, in many American cities and states. Boston, Chicago, New York, Philadelphia — and Michigan, Minnesota, Wisconsin, and California, for example — would be something other, and less, without their universities.

To discover and develop human talent is the aspiration of almost every nation in the modern world. It has been the historic American conviction, believed transferable in its benefits to the so-called "underdeveloped countries," that the existence of colleges and universities of many kinds and in great numbers assures a wide range and diversity of opportunity for talent development and political literacy, and that a greater flow of well-qualified youth to college is thereby bound to result.

Certainly this has been the American experience. Recent studies reveal that 30 to 35 per cent of the college-age group in the United States is now attending some type of post-secondary school institution — a figure that includes around 80 per cent of the highest-level graduates from our secondary schools. The geographic accessibility of American colleges and universities figures indispensably, of

42

course, in this record. The experience of the British civic universities has also demonstrated the great influence of proximity upon university attendance.

Since, unlike the British and Continental practice, there is in the United States no generally required examination system for the early identification of academically promising youth and for their later admission to most of the colleges and universities of our country, American high schools have had greater freedom to develop programs suited to the special needs of the huge numbers of non-college-going youth. This curricular freedom of the American secondary school has, however, come in lately for some serious criticism. And it must be acknowledged that one of several undoubted problems of our educational system is the differing standards and programs of secondary schools, resulting from the multiplicity and diversity of American higher educational institutions — with their own disparate standards of admission and academic performance.

Another problem is that economic resources, rarely adequate for education in any nation, are often used unwisely in the United States to establish and maintain many small and educationally insignificant institutions rather than to sustain and strengthen the smaller number of distinguished ones. Among the 1,886 colleges and universities listed in the 1956 Directory of the United States Office of Education, 905 were operating with an enrollment of fewer than 500 students each. Nearly half the colleges, that is, were in more instances than not too small and underfinanced for efficient operation.

Unquestionably, too, rigorous training for the students of highest academic competence may be sacrificed in some institutions in the effort to serve large numbers. The recent Rockefeller Brothers Fund Survey makes much of this point in its eloquent plea for educational reorganization to serve what it speaks of as "the pursuit of excellence." The American college degree, it must be admitted, varies in its attestation to academic achievement and integrity. The best graduate schools sometimes find difficult the evaluation of undergraduate college credentials and must rely increasingly on the so-called Graduate Record Examination or other tests for aid in this respect.

But there is more order than one might suppose in this seeming chaos. Voluntary but highly organized and stringent accreditation by regional educational and professional associations has accomplished in considerable degree what the British system was evolved to underwrite in the development and maintenance of standards. State departments of education may also participate in the process. In some states, the major state university has accrediting authority for other institutions. More than 75 per cent of all American institutions have received some type of accreditation — full, provisional or probationary, or "partial," that is, some units of the institution fully accredited, others not.

Indeed, accreditation by outside professional associations — such as law, medicine, social work, and engineering — had become at various stages so rigid and statistical as to be regarded as an interference with the freedom of the universities, which some years ago rebelled and organized a National Commission on Accrediting to restrain this outside interference — a kind of anomalous accrediting body to "accredit the accreditors"!

The pattern of local autonomy and democratic diversity that I have outlined in the establishment and development of American colleges and universities is in strong apparent contrast to the pattern of American university administration. Legally and theoretically in most universities — both state and private — the authority of lay boards of trustees, regents, and curators is absolute. Actually, it is largely unexercised except by delegation or in some rare crisis.

This system of lay trustees and boards of regents is unique in the whole world tradition of higher education. The ancient Alexandrian and the later Continental universities of the Middle Ages, Oxford and Cambridge, the great pre-World War I German universities — none of these had boards of control like ours. They were ruled mainly by guilds of students or teachers, or by the church or state. The foreign scholar finds our system hard to understand or approve, and many of our own scholars and scientists, steeped in the Old World academic tradition, are likewise skeptical. But it seems to me they debate the theory without appraising the practice. The thing to study and understand is not merely the fact of control, but the nature of its exercise.

American higher education was shaped primarily by the milieu of the expanding frontier, of productive agricultural pioneering, of the discovery and exploitation of rich natural resources, of inventive industry and business, of a buoyant sense of individual and "classless" opportunity. Paralleling these phenomena were the rise and spread in all parts of the country of schools, colleges, and universities, with an understandable emphasis upon the "usefulness" of knowledge, and with a reliance upon widely responsive private and public interest and support.

Lacking a true "teaching class" in the Massachusetts Bay Colony, the founders of Harvard created a board of overseers consisting of six clergymen and six magistrates as the controlling agency. The College of William and Mary, organized by royal charter in 1693, was launched likewise with a body of non-teachers as its governing board. Yale University began with ten clerical trustees, Princeton with a mixed governing body of religious ministers and laymen.

Thus lay, not academic, control of American higher education, and the exercise of lay authority through administrative delegation, became the characteristics of American university government which have endured to the present day.

As former Chancellor Samuel P. Capen of the University of Buffalo wrote in his book *The Management of Universities,* we see in our country "a simon-pure example of authoritarian government . . . a plan of university control, which technically and legally, does not show even a chemical trace of democracy!"

But actually the case is otherwise, he pointed out. After describing the defeated struggles of the professors in the early decades "to capture the authority over their institutions which they believed they were entitled to have and which their English colleagues exercised," Chancellor Capen observed:

"The American plan of institutional management is without doubt responsible for the prodigious and unparalleled spread of higher education in the United States, for the reason that it directs the attention of the hundreds of individual citizens who serve as [governing] board members to the advantages of a wide diffusion of educational opportunities. These citizens in turn help to create the public sentiment that finds expression in gifts and appropriations wholly unmatched in any other country.

"In particular, the concentration of executive authority inherent in the American plan facilitates the expansion of individual institutions and their quick adaptation to the changing demands of the society they serve."

Thus in a paradoxical way the apparently autocratic method of governing universities through boards of trustees and appointed administrators seems to have served our expanding democratic society better than government by majority vote of faculties and students in the European tradition. In a real sense, the American lay board of representative citizens is another evidence of the democratic instinct in our people.

The sound but strange fact is that American college and university boards of trustees have come to regard themselves truly as *trustees* — not boards of managers. They have recognized the fact that, unlike the directors of business and industrial enterprises, they are called upon to govern an enterprise whose major and most significant tasks they could not possibly themselves perform, or in some cases even understand, for lack of the intensive specialized training involved. To be sure, the corporate and statutory and constitutional powers of the trustees are virtually absolute, but they have largely delegated these powers to the administration and faculty. They have enforced the principle of accountability rather than authority.

Whenever this principle is seriously transgressed — and there are enough occasional glaring exceptions to illuminate the rule — there is trouble, and the college in question is deeply disadvantaged. The truest function of trustees, and it is a critical and difficult one, is to stand firmly as lay interpreters and defenders of the college or university's high purposes and function in the larger civic community; to see and protect the difference between long-range public service and short-range public servility.

As Chancellor Capen also wrote, "Educational administration is a necessary institutional function. . . its sole purpose is to facilitate the processes of teaching and research, and to promote improvements in these processes." Operationally, it is to and through the college or university president — aided by deans and other fellow-administrators, advised and admonished by component college faculties and university-wide senates and faculty committees — that the legally all-powerful boards of trustees delegate and exercise most of their managerial powers.

To the faculties, however, is definitely delegated in the typical American university constitution the management of academic affairs. Here I refer to the requirements for admission and degrees; the formulation of curricular policies; recommendations, through the president, for the employment, assignment, and promotion of academic staff, and their compensation within budgetary limits determined by the trustees and administration; and the like.

"Administration" is a clearly recognized function of American university government, coordinate with but not subordinate to "academic duties." It is held responsible in two directions. The president is the executive officer of the lay trustees, and likewise the head of the faculty. He is the spokesman and interpreter of each to the other. It is expected that he will meet the requirements both of institutional leadership and of educational statesmanship. His task is not a simple or an easy one. He must mobilize, coordinate, and integrate faculty participation, trustee influence and support, and public and private response to the needs and purposes of the university.

So large an assignment and so great a responsibility may seem unrealistic to observers from abroad. It may seem to present an astonishing contrast with the situation, for example, in the British universities; and British writers have charged that in the United States many professors take little interest in the general policy of their university. But the contrast is over-accentuated, I think. The American university administrator is constantly in close communication and consultation with his faculty — regularly through his deans and faculty committees, and often individually. He is sup-

47

ported in his duties by a considerable corps of associate administrators, thus diffusing widely the exercise of authority. In most cases, both he and they have been faculty members themselves, remaining sensitive to professorial sentiment and morale.

Indeed, we would seriously misinterpret the function of educational administration in the United States if we failed to note the evolution of the American university presidency into a developmental rather than an operational office. It is in the American tradition for the president to become himself the initiator, the catalyzer, and the energizer of teaching duties. In this respect he may be compared with the many eminent headmasters of British secondary schools. The history of higher education in the United States takes large account of such presidential leaders as Wayland of Brown, Gilman of Johns Hopkins, Eliot and Conant of Harvard, Harper and Hutchins of Chicago, Butler of Columbia, Van Hise of Wisconsin, White of Cornell, Jordan of Stanford.

The faculties and their deans, with their control of the curriculum and staff appointments, remain of course the true determinants of institutional destiny, and the real overlords of what goes on, day to day, in the lives of the students. The American student may sometimes envy the greater autonomy of students in European universities and deride the limited function of his own "student government." But in American universities, and especially in state universities, student government, like faculty government, operates under a partial and delegated grant of authority. The "sovereignty" to which many student leaders seem instinctively to aspire is an unrealistic goal, conceded to no other group or officer in the university's body-politic and inconsistent with the interdependent nature of the university enterprise.

Those officially charged with university government, year after year, must live with their decisions long after any given student generation has departed the scene. Students do not stay long enough to test out their experiments, or to live with them responsibly in the long range. The university, moreover — particularly the state university — while so often spoken of as a "community of scholars," is not the kind of political community that we know in a village, a city, or a state. It is far from self-contained. Its citizens levy no taxes upon themselves. Its administrators are responsible to two constituencies: the university community itself and the larger, supporting community of the state. The intellectual autonomy of universities we cherish and seek to safeguard, but there is no fiscal or political autonomy, especially in the publicly supported institutions.

None of the groups in the American university community — the trustees, the administration, the faculty, or the students — is self-contained or, in practice, fully self-governing. Each has responsibilities to the other; each needs communication and cooperation with the other; each is sometimes dissatisfied with its place in the sphere of things. As in any democratic enterprise, the problems of government, including university government, are never quite resolved. But the basic relationship remains a cooperative and not an autocratic one, emphasizing the voluntary nature of the university enterprise, in which any form of arbitrary administration is incompatible with success.

The aims of scholarship and science, of the advancement of learning and the search for truth, are the university's reason for being; and university administration, no matter what its particular form of organization, exists to serve those ends. Not as *primus inter pares* but as *servus servorum* the American university administrator regards himself. In relation to his fellows of the faculties, he discerns the duty of productive partnership, realizing as President Eliot of Harvard wrote, that "learning is always republican . . . it has idols, but not masters."

# CHAPTER V

# Academic Freedom and Responsibility

Universities the world over, no matter what their differences in tradition and administration, have been citadels of freedom, of disinterested intelligence and good will. The menace of political and economic absolutism and the mass mind they, above all other institutions, have resisted and must continue to resist — standing as islands of reason in an excited world, maintaining freedom even against the forces of popular pressure upon occasion.

In this country, the ideal of intellectual freedom has been as basic an American tenet as free enterprise in our economic life. Both are part of the pattern under which our American system has developed: the ideal of "elbow room" for individual initiative in a national climate of self-reliance; and the ideal of personal freedom — socially responsible and restrained, to be sure; "liberty under law," as we say; but freedom in the sense of the right to think, and do, and grow in our own way and our own work.

The place of education in this system is all important, and, rightly, it is everybody's business. Historically, education has been an instrument of national policy in the United States. There is no mention of it in either the Declaration of Independence or the Constitution, but it was the imperishable mandate of the Ordinance of 1787 that schools and the means of education shall be forever encouraged.

Education is indispensable to every hope for the survival of democracy, the nation's founders declared again and again. Washington, in his Farewell Address, urged, "Promote, then, as an object of primary importance, institutions for the general diffusion of knowledge." James Madison proposed to the Constitutional Convention that Congress be empowered to establish a national university. Jefferson's lifelong preoccupation with education culminated in his founding of the University of Virginia. John Quincy Adams earnestly admonished the public to support "scientific research and inquiry" toward "the improvement of agriculture, commerce and manufactures, the cultivation and encouragement of the mechanic and the elegant arts, the advancement of literature, and the progress of the sciences, ornamental and profound."

This unquestioning faith in education is as national as the Stars and Stripes. But the desire to make education a major instrument of national policy has its dangers. It is something different today from the broad and general purposes of the founders, and among many thoughtful educators it is the cause of grave concern.

Let me speak plainly: Never in my almost forty years of university work have there been so many people trying to tell the colleges and universities what, or what not, to teach as in these postwar years. This pressure comes from government, and from organized business and industry; it comes from organized labor, from the tyrannical mass mind of powerful political majorities, from earnest and excited, fearful and prejudiced citizens in public life and private.

I am concerned about this pressure, because to my mind the last stronghold of all freedom is intellectual freedom. I am concerned to know whether Gresham's Law applies in education — the ancient tendency for the less valuable money to drive out of circulation the more valuable, as Sir Thomas patiently explained to the bewildered Queen Elizabeth nearly four hundred years ago. Commenting on Gresham's Law, Charles L. Prather, in his elementary text *Money and Banking*, remarked that "it seems a strange contradiction that while in most lines the best articles capture the market, in the case of money alone the poor is preferred to the good as a medium of exchange." In education we must have a currency of knowledge in which the good will drive out the bad — and this will prevail only in the climate of freedom of a dynamic and democratic social order and economy.

In his thoughtful book *The Ramparts We Guard*, Professor R. M. MacIver of Columbia University wrote that "democracy is the only system of government that trusts in its own persuasiveness . . . the only system that has faith in the free mind . . . the only system that does not make education the servant of power." And it is interesting to remember that Karl Marx said much the same thing a hundred years ago when he wrote that the only effective opponent of Russia's march to world power was "the explosive power of democratic ideas, and the inborn urge in the direction of human freedom."

The recent pressures on colleges and universities are understandable only if America has now come to regard education as an instrument of national policy in the way that Hitler, Mussolini, and Stalin regarded it — as a kind of Procrustean bed to break or bend the wills and minds of youth and their teachers to some single and inflexible pattern. As a university president, I believe that any American institution of higher learning which tolerates on its faculty the presence of a proved or self-confessed Communist betrays the trust and the tradition of intellectual freedom; yet at the same time, with former President James B. Conant of Harvard, equally I believe that in the free market of ideas which universities above all must provide and protect, the Soviet doctrine cannot "stand up for a moment against the devastating analysis of those who start from other points of view."

As former Chief Justice Hughes of the United States Supreme Court has written: "The greater the importance of safeguarding the community from incitements to the overthrow of our institutions by force and violence, the more imperative is the need to preserve inviolate the constitutional rights of free speech, free press and free assembly in order to maintain the opportunity for free political discussion, to the end that government may be responsive to the will of the people and that changes, if desired, may be obtained by peaceful means."

Colleges and universities, by reason of their historic ideals, must be especially concerned with maintaining these freedoms in a social and political climate that has lately been increasingly intolerant of them. Charges of "communism in the colleges" have recently been a nationwide issue, affecting both publicly and privately supported institutions and requiring college presidents to mediate the conflict between frightened and hysterical, sometimes sinister but more often sincere, public attitudes and an inescapable obligation to the principle of academic freedom. Much too often, the vexing issue of communism on the campus has been made the excuse for a kind of coercion far transcending that problem. The proved patriotism of those in the teaching profession has been impugned unjustly, eroding the autonomy of the institutions they serve and thus depriving the nation of the very service it needs most — which is the advancement of learning and the untrammeled search for truth.

Educators were concerned and alarmed by the threat of federal intimidation and control implicit in the introduction in the United States Senate in 1950 of a resolution directing the Senate Committee on Education and Labor to make a full and complete investigation of all phases of subversive propaganda in the public schools, colleges, and universities of the various states. I was alarmed, too, when earlier a House committee demanded a list of textbooks used in the colleges of this country, both public and private. I was alarmed because I remembered the Nazi odor of burning books, and the Communist proscription of any ideas but those authorized by the Politburo, with its iron hand upon the minds of men.

I am still concerned by the rash of so-called "loyalty oaths" which a frightened public has seemed minded to impose upon professors as a special class, through pressure-sensitive congressmen and state legislators and even through trustees and regents forgetful of their special duty to protect and encourage the high potential of intellectual freedom. (I do not, of course, refer to or protest against federal precautions to protect the safety and security of atomic and other research for military purposes.)

These oaths are understandable, I suppose, if we imagine that the college professor can control the attitudes of youth. But what about newspaper editors, preachers, radio commentators, motion-picture writers, and all the others who have enormous impact upon the youthful mind? No loyalty oaths are required of them. They would fight such a proposal to the death, and rightly so. Loyalty is a voluntary thing, freely given; it cannot be commanded or coerced; it can only be invited and encouraged, its generous meaning made plain. The negative oath, denying disloyalty, is even less effective. It will catch no Communist, whose code is commitment to deceit and deception, to concealment and the cold disregard of any conception of conscience.

It is unfair, and a stultifying thing, to subject teachers as a special class to such a test — because, as Professor Max Radin wrote in a discussion of the loyalty oath controversy at the University of California, "to ask any person to declare that he has not committed a specific wrongful act carries an implication that he is suspected." Certainly no banker or public official would feel it right that he be made to swear to the federal or state examiners that he had embezzled no funds.

The issue of academic freedom concerns the teacher more directly than any other member of the university community — for the classic definition of a professor is a person "who thinks otherwise"! Democracy needs the dissenter, and the campus is his logical habitat in its ceaseless quest for new knowledge and ideas and the search for truth. But with freedom goes responsibility, and this is a time, I think, to reassess the meaning of both academic freedom and responsibility.

If academic freedom seems some "eternal verity" sprung full-blown from the very nature of learning, let us look back and remember Galileo atop the leaning tower, the two stones of unequal weight in his outstretched hands. Below him is the medieval world, confident in its knowledge, obsessed with its systems. How strange to remember the outcries when Galileo let fall those stones to discover for himself if the heavier did in truth — as Aristotle said — fall the faster.

The medieval man had no concept of academic freedom. He had none because he needed none. In his classic history of the German university, Friedrich Paulsen wrote: "The older university instruction was everywhere based upon the assumption that the truth had already been given, that instruction had to do with transmission only, and that it was the duty of the controlling authorities to see to it that no false doctrines were taught." But, he continued, "the new university instruction began with the assumption that the truth must be discovered."

In that statement — "the truth must be discovered" — is the beginning of modern science and humanism, and of our notions of the meaning of academic freedom. The truth must be *discovered*; and those who would travel the road toward the unknown must be free.

When Galileo came down from the tower, having proved that Aristotle was a better friend than master (the stones having reached the ground simultaneously), he found that while he had his truth, he did not have his freedom. He faced the spirit of the ancient inquisition, the passion of prejudice, the stubbornness of those who will not learn and have no wish to learn — and all these are yet alive despite the unfolding enlightenment of the later centuries. There is now, as then, the often unconscious feeling of antagonism toward those who, by reason or for any reason, would disturb the happy inertia of the complacent or the vested interests of the status quo.

The principle of freedom for the scholar is simple in statement but difficult in application. The modern university must give the scholar a protected freedom to do his work, but it cannot build a wall around him, or insulate him from the rest of the world. Universities are social agencies. To the extent that they study society, they move into its center of action. The principles of Milton, Hume, Rousseau, and Locke goaded the minds of men of action — Adams and Jefferson, among others; they flowered in the development of our American democracy with its ideals of freedom, justice, the inviolate integrity of the individual.

The scholar, therefore, is no recluse; the university is no place of refuge from social, individual, or institutional responsibility. Our accepted American code of academic freedom and tenure fails to take sufficient and realistic account of this consideration, it seems to me. Indeed, in my long association with university life, I have seen as many professorial betrayals of the deeper principles of academic freedom and responsibility as instances of their violation by presidents and governing boards.

Yet considering the full range of American college and university experience, these exceptions have been infinitesimally few. The scholarly profession as a whole seems to me one of the most innately conservative forces in society. Just try to change a curriculum! There is no greater understanding of tradition, no more devoted allegiance to the things proved good and true, than among scholars. For every old truth they discard, they cling to a thousand others.

But if inner self-discipline, devotion to the disinterested pursuit of truth, and freedom from coercion from his own or anyone else's preconceptions be the mark and the responsibility of the scholar, then let the members of the scholarly and teaching professions create some machinery for their enforcement upon themselves.

There is no such machinery now. The code of academic freedom and tenure is completely clear in respect to the obligation of presidents and trustees; but it imposes, as a code of procedure, no similar obligation upon the professor and gives little more than lip service to any self-imposed or group-enforced compliance with the criteria of responsible scholarship. As things stand now, academic freedom becomes an issue ex post facto, after some administrator or board of trustees has been charged by the complainant with its abrogation.

The philosophy of liberty, transmuted through the university environment, must receive special and more circumscribed interpretation. It carries a special obligation. Historically, the constitutional autonomy the state university enjoys is more than fiscal or managerial; it is moral, related to our special function in society; it imposes a peculiar restraint. Institutionally, each of us has an accountability for the protection of the other's freedom, which is *academic* — not political — freedom. There is a difference, not sufficiently recognized it seems to me.

The recent waves of international immorality must have made us all more aware of the need for ethical integrity in every individual and every profession. Men and women of the academic world, I believe, are closer to unity and common sense on this issue than ever before. We understand that clever dialectic is not intelligence; that responsibility is the core, not the curtailment, of freedom.

An overwhelming majority of the academic profession has decided, I am sure, that a true totalitarian cannot possibly be a true scholar; that membership in the Communist party betrays the trust and tradition of intellectual freedom, means that the search for truth has been abandoned to dogma and deceit. Yet the academic profession has failed — at the national level, at least — to work out any procedure for policing its own members in this area of public anxiety. It has not formally revised or repudiated the report of the American Association of University Professors' Committee on Academic Freedom and Tenure, published in 1948, which argued that membership in the Communist party must not necessarily, or *ipso facto,* disqualify faculty members or deprive them of protection against dismissal.

My own concern about any possible infiltration of education by communism — and the danger, I think, is long past — is not that it might produce subversive saboteurs or scientists who will give away atomic secrets. So far as I know, no American professor has been indicted, tried, and found guilty, under due process, of treason or espionage. The danger is that any such infiltration could erode the ethics and integrity of intellectual freedom and independence.

It was for this reason that without reservation I subscribed, together with the thirty-six other presidents of the institutions comprising the Association of American Universities, to the statement which declared that present membership in the Communist party is in itself sufficient proof of lack of fitness to be a member of the academic community of scholars; that the doctrinaire discipline of the Communist party and intellectual freedom are a contradiction in terms, are antithetical.

We shall cling, of course, to our conviction that there is a distinction between the unpopular and the undemocratic. We shall recognize the duty of the university administration and governing board and the teaching profession, acknowledging their mutual responsibilities, to maintain and defend the exercise of independent thought, indispensable for their own survival and the survival of the society they serve.

Let us remember, too, that the ideas which have saved civilizations from stagnation and decay have always been "subversive" in the sense that they overturn our prejudices and preconceptions. In science, in economics, and in politics that has been so. It is the glory of democracy to provide the arena for the struggle of ideas, and thereby for advance through peaceful evolution rather than through the violence of revolution. "A clash of doctrines is not a disaster — it is an opportunity," the philosopher Alfred North Whitehead has said. There is no safer place for their clash than in universities where the instinct of disinterested analysis and of relentless criticism is deeply ingrained.

But it is also important to remember, as President Coffman of Minnesota once wrote, "that the schools of a democracy are not forums for the spread of doctrine, and that the classrooms are not arenas for the promotion of any particular social theories." So I likewise would urge, believing, again with President Coffman, that "there should be a ferment in every university — not political, not social, not religious — but a ferment arising from an inner urge to learn, to interpret, to discover new knowledge. The unrest in a university should be the unrest of scholarship concerned with achievement, with mastery, with understanding, and with wisdom."

Education in the academic environment of intellectual freedom is no dead-leveler. It makes for *inequality* — as Felix Schelling said, "the inequality of individuality; the inequality of success; the glorious inequality of talent, of genius. For inequality, not mediocrity — individual superiority, not standardization — is the measure of progress of the world."

Freedom in education and research makes room for the development of individuality. Science and scholarship, inventive and resourceful, are the catalysts of change — the means to an expanding economy, a dynamic democracy, and a better life. The wonders of scientific advance are the fruits of a free society, which world events in recent years should have made plain no nation can take for granted. There is a good deal of security in freedom — but no security for freedom, history shows.

The survival of a free society depends upon free intelligence: intelligence free to explore and discover, to reinterpret in a changing time and world our heritage of freedom, and to redesign its development in the time to come. This means scientific freedom, intellectual freedom, academic freedom — the freedom of schools and colleges and universities to do their indispensable job. It means freedom from the kind of "anti-intellectualism" which has become a fashion in some circles, freedom from the demagogue's derision of the "egghead." It means heeding Goethe's warning that there is nothing more frightful than ignorance in action.

Whatever threatens education's freedom — its freedom of thought and inquiry — threatens all freedom. Organized education, our colleges and universities, especially our state universities, with their personnel capable of prosecuting research and of finding, encouraging, and training students competent to carry it forward — these institutions above all others in our society, it seems to me, are the trustees of freedom. The prospects of our free society are almost boundless if we can perceive and protect the genius of freedom: freedom for discovery and diversity, for change and advance.

# CHAPTER VI

# The Place of Religion in a State University

ALONG with individual and academic freedom, the principle of "separation of church and state" is precious in our American heritage. None of us holding responsibility for the control or administration of state-supported higher education would knowingly or willfully violate this fundamental concept.

At the same time, however, the interrelationships of religion and education — of the home, the church, and the school — are also part of the American tradition. They have a firm hold on the minds and hearts of our people. They were attested in the beginnings of the nation in that historic Ordinance of 1787 to which I have referred so often. In establishing the Northwest Territory of which Minnesota was a part, the Ordinance laid down the mandate that since "religion, morality, and knowledge [are] necessary to good government and the happiness of mankind, schools and the means of education shall forever be encouraged."

The apparent conflict between these two principles in our American tradition has contributed to an aroused public interest in the relationship of church and state today and the place of religion in public education. Within recent years, at least three new books have been published in this country dealing with the doctrine of separation of church and state. Attendance at three "Institutes on Religion in the State Universities," conducted by the University of Minnesota beginning in 1949, demonstrated the anxious desire among educators and religious leaders to discover some modus vivendi between objective and impartial scholarship, as a teaching function of the state university, and proper response to the obvious needs of young people for religious guidance and activity within their experience as students and within the university climate of total — including extracurricular — learning.

Most important of all recent developments in this area of controversy have been at least three decisions of the United States Supreme Court in cases appealed from the lower courts arising from taxpayer suits relating to religion in the public schools. State universities have also experienced litigation in this field. With respect to religion, anything that is undertaken or not undertaken by state universities — whether it be religious teaching, activity, or critical analysis — becomes the subject of heated controversy.

Accordingly, the University of Minnesota, which in the past has been unfairly criticized as a "godless institution," has more recently been under legal attack for the opposite fault in a suit alleging the illegality of various policies: our cooperation with neighborhood churches and religious foundations; our permitting use of university buildings by student groups for religious activities; our appointment, on the staff of the dean of students, of a coordinator of students' religious activities; our custom of invocations and benedictions at university ceremonies; our traditional baccalaureate services at commencement time; and the like. The details of this lawsuit may be of cautionary interest to other tax-supported colleges and universities.

On June 5, 1951, W. L. Sholes, a Minneapolis attorney, filed suit in court against the University of Minnesota, petitioning for an alternative writ of mandamus. Sholes asked the court to require the regents of the university to adopt immediately rules and regulations prohibiting all use of University of Minnesota property and facilities for the teaching or disseminating of any and all "sectarian religious doctrine," prohibiting the use of university prop-

61

erty and facilities in aiding "or even permitting" any religious activities on the campus, "except such as are purely secular in nature and are essential to a better understanding of literature, science and the arts." The university was accused of violating through its support of religious activities not only its own charter, but also the Minnesota Constitution, the First and Fourteenth Amendments to the Constitution of the United States, and the United States Code Annotated relating to civil rights.

Our defending regents maintained, among other things, that since they are the constitutionally independent governing body of the university, no person has any right to seek a remedy for such a grievance in court before giving the regents an opportunity to consider and act upon the complaint.

Substantially agreeing with the university position, the trial judge decided in favor of the university. The case was appealed to the Minnesota Supreme Court, which affirmed on May 2, 1952, the trial or district court decision — on basically the same grounds. The decision is now final, as no review in the United States Supreme Court was sought.

The university is no longer "on the griddle." But we are still sitting in an uncomfortably warm position. For at any time Mr. Sholes *et al.* are free to bring the entire matter before the board of regents, and of course the board will not deny a hearing. The case was won on frankly technical grounds, but the issue is still very much alive and has yet to be tried on its merits.

We at the University of Minnesota were accused of a great many things — many of the allegations being, as the trial judge put it, "broad, general and somewhat nebulous." We wondered, naturally, if we had been selected for attack because of practices outstandingly different from those of the average land-grant institution. Therefore, each of seventy-four land-grant and other state universities and colleges was sent a questionnaire asking rather specific questions on current practices with regard to religious activities. We received sixty-five responses from the seventy-four questionnaires, which in itself is indicative of the lively interest in the subject.

What did we find out? Just about what we had expected — that the overwhelming majority of publicly supported colleges and universities were at least as active as the University of Minnesota in supporting religious activities among students. Approximately nine out of ten of the responding institutions provide university space for the business, social, and discussion meetings of denominational groups or "Y" associations. About the same number assist religious organizations in obtaining a census of religious preferences or affiliations of students and hold special convocations emphasizing religious subjects.

Three out of four state universities hold baccalaureate services on university property. The same number have a chaplain or in some degree similar staff members, either appointed by the university or subject to its approval, to encourage and work with students on religious participation. A great majority (two-thirds) provide religious or "Y" groups with office space, and likewise provide them with space for worship services conducted by denominational religious leaders supplied by outside religious organizations.

Less common is the practice of appointing a university-paid staff member with responsibility for the direct sponsorship and administration of student religious activities. About half of the questionnaires reported such appointments; the same number indicated that space is provided for religious counseling by denominational religious leaders from outside religious organizations. Only one state university in three provides chapels or other meeting places designed or designated especially for religious services. Only one in seven *requires* students to supply their religious preferences or affiliations.

Evidently we have here a wide spectrum of practices — ranging from a nearly "hands-off" position to one of direct participation in the religious instruction of students, for several of our correspondents reported active departments of religion. Others wrote that courses in religion taught off-campus by denominational religious leaders were being accepted for full academic credit.

The median practice seems to be one of rather well-coordinated administrative encouragement and assistance to voluntary student religious activities, with no serious attempt on the part of the university or college itself to offer its own religious program.

On the University of Minnesota campuses, religious activities are included among many so-called "extracurricular" student activities; and these, we believe, are important in the total educational experience of our students. We think of these activities as part of the learning process, and we think of them as "co-curricular" rather than "extracurricular" (which is something more than merely a semantic distinction). The university has no academic department of religion, but in quite a few subjects and courses, our professors do, I'm sure, help to reduce religious illiteracy — and the conversion of illiteracy to literacy in any field, of course, is a prime objective of the university. But literacy is not the same thing as faith, and faith is the province of the churches.

The University of Minnesota as such conducts no religious program of its own. It legally could not do so, we believe; and even if it wished to, it could not hope to muster the diverse religious resources which the various churches and faiths offer in abundance, each in its own cherished way, without university direction or interference.

The core of our policy at the University of Minnesota is found in the strong encouragement of, and cooperation with, independent religious foundations which are not controlled by the university, but are supported by the interested denominations; and in the approval of student religious organizations, encouraged, assisted, and counseled by the staff of the dean of students. It is to carry out this policy that the university has established in the office of the dean of students the special position of "coordinator of student religious activities."

The constitution of the university explicitly forbids any religious test to determine the acceptability of its students and staff members. The official admission forms of the university bear no indication of race, religious creed, or color. The religious preference cards used at registration time provide space for the student to indicate his religious belief, if he chooses, but it is made plain that the return of this card to the university is voluntary. The university hopes that all students will fill out these cards and return them, so that they may be turned over to the appropriate foundation or church. But neither the cards nor records of them are kept by the university. In collecting them, the university seeks to be helpful not only to the foundations and churches, but primarily to the new students who need the friendship and guidance that the religious agencies can give.

The accusations brought in court against us — and I use the pronoun in its broad implication, because most state universities are engaging in similar practices — are, basically, that the practices I have just described violate the United States Constitution. Let us refresh our memories, therefore, with the pertinent passages from the Constitution which are cited against us. The First Amendment says, in part: "Congress shall make no law respecting an establishment of religion, or prohibiting the free exercise thereof . . ." The Fourteenth Amendment enjoins that "No state shall make or enforce any law which shall abridge the privileges and immunities of citizens of the United States . . ."

The territorial law of Minnesota which founded the university is more specific, stating that "no sectarian instruction shall be allowed in such University." Likewise is the Minnesota Constitution more specific: ". . . nor shall any man be compelled to attend, erect or support any place of worship, or to maintain any religious or ecclesiastical ministry, against his consent . . . nor shall any money be drawn from the treasury for the benefit of any religious societies, or religious or theological seminaries . . ."

Clearly the drafters of both the federal Constitution and many of the state constitutions were anxious to maintain the principle of separation of church and state. But even their most specific language is susceptible of broadly differing interpretations.

For example, what *is* "sectarian instruction"? The Supreme Court of the United States is the only body which can decide, under our system of government, which is the proper interpretation of any point of constitutional language. And with the passages that bear on religion they have had singular difficulty. This is emphasized in a paragraph from Justice Robert H. Jackson's concurring opinion in the McCollum case:

"The task of separating the secular from the religious in education is one of magnitude, intricacy and delicacy. . . . It is idle to pretend that this task is one for which we can find in the Constitution one word to help us as judges to decide where the secular ends and the sectarian begins in education. Nor can we find guidance in any other legal source. It is a matter on which we can find no law but our own prepossessions. . . ."

The celebrated McCollum decision seemed to imply a rigid, doctrinaire attitude of the Supreme Court. The heart of this decision was contained in this sentence (the italics are mine): "Neither [a state nor the federal government] can pass laws which aid one religion, *aid all religions*, or prefer one religion over another." But on two occasions since the McCollum decision the Supreme Court has expressed itself further and somewhat differently on the matter.

One was the Doremus case of 1952 in which the court refused to review a decision of the New Jersey Supreme Court upholding a public-school Bible-reading statute, because the complaining parties did not show they were in any way harmed by the practice under attack. The court expressly ruled that a taxpayer cannot raise the constitutional question unless he shows that the challenged practice has a genuine effect upon the taxpayer's financial interests. According to some of my lawyer friends, the most probable effect of the Doremus case is that it will tend to make more unlikely the interference with present practices at state universities by the Supreme Court. At the same time, they tell me, it would probably not bar an attack on the payment of salaries for those officials of the university devoting substantial time to religious activities. Nor would it bar an attack on the practice of providing funds for the construction or maintenance of buildings or rooms used for a substantial period of time for religious activities without compensation to the university.

The second occasion was the Zorach v. Clauson decision of April 1952, which my legal friends describe as a "mellowing and softening" of the court's attitude toward cooperation of the state with religious organizations. More important than the exact ruling itself is the change in emphasis and attitude by the majority of eight from the rigid position on the McCollum case. The majority opinion, written by Justice William O. Douglas, illuminates this less rigid attitude:

"We are a religious people, whose institutions presuppose a Supreme Being. We guarantee the freedom to worship as one chooses. . . . We sponsor an attitude on the part of government that shows no partiality to any one group and that lets each flourish according to the zeal of its adherents and the appeal of its dogma. When the state encourages religious instruction or cooperates with religious authorities by adjusting the schedule of public events to sectarian needs, it follows the best of our traditions."

Nevertheless, the court evidently did not intend by its decision in the Zorach case to knock down the high wall separating church and state, for Justice Douglas went on: "Government may not finance religious groups nor undertake religious instruction nor blend secular and sectarian education nor use secular institutions to force one or some religion on any person."

Even so, Justice Douglas concluded: "But we find no constitutional requirement which makes it necessary for government to be hostile to religion and to throw its weight against efforts to widen the effective scope of religious influence. . . ."

Apparently the court has somewhat changed opinion since the McCollum decision and the ensuant storm of debate and protest. The point was made in public and even legal comments that should the McCollum decision be followed to its logical conclusion, we must suspend prayers in our legislative halls, perhaps even the phrase "so help me God" in our courtroom oaths. Indeed, the Supreme Court itself might have to commence its sessions without the traditional invocation to the Almighty.

What does this analysis of the Supreme Court's position mean to us? Must we proceed warily, keeping in mind that the principle of the separation of church and state remains the law of the land, and that at some point the Supreme Court may be forced to step in and say: "This is where we draw the line"? We may still antici-pate, I think, that the board of trustees or regents of some one of our state institutions may be petitioned to cease and desist all sup-port of religious activities on the campus. Reasoning from the University of Minnesota case, any such board will be well advised to review carefully its own policies, responding with open mind to any such petitioners.

A few things seem clear. There can be no sectarian or denomina-tional favoritism in cooperation with the churches, and no element of compulsion. The use of taxpayers' money to provide staff or space may be still an undecided issue, depending on the nature of the staff member's duties and the kind of uses made by religious groups of university rooms and buildings.

Seemingly it is wiser if the state university sponsors no program of its own of religious teaching or organized religious activity among students, but rather offers only its encouragement, assist-ance, and cooperation to programs sponsored by the students themselves as members of the various faiths under guidance of their own churches and religious leaders.

And yet, as educators, as administrators of institutions deeply committed to the aim of training for citizenship, we are well aware that knowledge alone is not enough. "The advancement of learn-ing and the search for truth" is more than an intellectual enter-prise — it is also a moral and spiritual one. We realize that it is the uses of knowledge that determine its worth; that except as intelli-gence is governed by ethical imperatives, it can be dangerous and destructive; that it is the lesson of human history and experience that religion has been proved best fitted to implant and inspire these ethical imperatives.

The regents and administration of the University of Minnesota keenly appreciate our obligation not only to comply with the basic American tenet of separation of church and state, but to set an ex-ample of compliance. We believe our activities to be completely consistent with the intention of the laws. Our cooperation with the churches, the foundations, and religious organizations is not a mat-ter of reluctant acquiescence, but one of thoughtful, purposeful, and nondenominational partnership in an educational philosophy and principle. The secular and legal charter of the university precludes any religious test of faculty and students, and prohibits any single sectarian approach to religious education; but it does not and was not meant to preclude encouragement and assistance to the concept of religious freedom, the freedom of religious choice and activity, the building of moral and social responsibility, and the influence of religious organizations in the lives of our students.

Stated affirmatively, we *do* believe that creation of the office of the coordinator of religious affairs at the University of Minnesota, and the building with privately raised funds of an all-faith chapel on the campus of the Pennsylvania State University, and the presentation of a concert of sacred music in Rackham Hall on the campus of the University of Michigan, are acts not only in compliance with the laws of the United States and of the states involved, but faithful to the historic American unity of "religion, morality, and knowledge."

In all conscience, we cannot be neutral to the major issue of our time. "The world today," as Clarence H. Tuttle has said, "is divided as between our own Declaration of Independence, constituting the 'faith of our fathers' that the natural rights of man come from the Creator — and the Marxian declaration that they come from the state; and hence what the state grants today, it can withdraw tomorrow."

In that conflict, even the so-called "godless state university" of outworn opprobrium cannot stand mute. Nor is it likely, so it seems to me, that its non-sectarian, non-compulsory religious endeavors can fail to be sustained by its citizen constituency — the mothers and fathers and neighbors of our students — or, indeed, by the highest courts of our land.

# CHAPTER VII

# *Athletics: Colleges or Clubs?*

I f the place of religion in the state university is a difficult and still not finally solved problem, so too — in perhaps a less serious but equally controversial way — is the question of the proper place of athletics in the larger scheme of the university's purpose. Perhaps it is not a "less serious" question after all, when coaches are still hanged in effigy and hounded into resignation, when some athletic staff members callously practice and condone illegal and unethical recruiting, and when many judge the greatness of a university by its record of victories on the athletic fields.

I will be blunt: Without a doubt American intercollegiate athletics have gotten out of hand. They have become infested with commercialization and professionalism, sapping to a considerable degree the fine ideals they exemplify. The job now is to reverse these trends, without throwing out the baby with the bath. College sports and professional athletics both have their rightful place — but we must remember that they are different. What goes on or should go on in a big-time college football stadium is not the same as in a major league baseball park.

The present trend toward more subsidization of athletic team members, through athletic scholarship plans, for example, tends to blur the line between professional and amateur sport. This is most evident in football. I have no quarrel with professional football.

It is frankly and openly "play for pay," just like professional base-ball. It will give the spectator more scoring and a higher degree of skill than college football. Intercollegiate football, on the other hand, will show more spirit and more sportsmanship — and I think it is these last which college men and women want to see, and which colleges want to encourage.

It was originally from the British, with their emphasis on ama-teurism, that we inherited the ideal of sportsmanship, and we acknowledge this when we say that something is "cricket" or "not cricket." Beyond this, Americans have built into sports something of our own that we shall lose at our peril: the American spirit of hustle, resourcefulness, fierce but fair competition, and the will to win.

If we admire teamwork, stamina, and the courage to fight on against odds, let us remember these are things the athlete learns for himself and teaches all the rest of us vicariously. They are prop-er and appropriate educational objectives; but we must come to them with clean hands and a sense of educational perspective. The lesson of generous and sacrificial loyalty to something bigger and finer than ourselves is one that is taught in athletics. It is one we cannot neglect if we are to survive and surpass the strange and twisted claim of the Communist creed in a divided world.

But the heart of this lesson, and the controlling criterion of col-lege sports, must be the amateur ideal. Under this concept, the paid player is a professional. Professional sports are played to put money into the pockets of their sponsors, the club owners and in-vestors. College athletics may make money, too, but not for the profit of individuals (except in a few strange and indefensible cases where coaches share in the gate receipts). Nearly always the finan-cial returns are re-invested in expanded physical education and recreational facilities for the whole student body.

With the professional player, competition is a legitimate voca-tion; with the amateur, it is avocation. Both types of sport, pro-fessional and amateur, attract large crowds, provide commendable recreation, collect large receipts, and have their appropriate place in American life. But their aims and ethics are different. They are

71

played, and judged, and enjoyed under different standards; and the difference is generally well understood.

Most of the college conference athletic codes make that difference abundantly clear, in theory at least. If it has become blurred in practice, then the need is to clear it up and bring the picture back into focus. Not only clarity but courage is required. The right conduct of intercollegiate athletics stands in need today not of more lip service, but of good faith and stronger support. High ideals, and their formal expression in rules and regulations, require in addition the firm purpose and the machinery to enforce them.

The National Collegiate Athletic Association, in adopting its athletic codes and in providing for their enforcement, has sought to set amateur and educational standards. But the NCAA is so large, and must meet the needs and varying policies of so many different kinds of colleges and universities, that its regulations can hardly be considered more than a "least common denominator" of athletic reform. It is at this point that the various intercollegiate conferences, like our Western Conference, can start toward something better and can set sound examples of the best.

There are three sets of rules to which the college athletic administration and coaches and teams are responsible. There are the rules of "eligibility," which require team members to meet scholastic standards, to be satisfactory students. There are the rules of the game, which define infractions on the field of play and impose penalties. There are the rules concerning recruitment and subsidy of players, as enacted by the NCAA and the various intercollegiate athletic conferences.

The faculty of any college or university can be depended upon to enforce the rules of scholastic eligibility. Referees, umpires, and other such officials are specially provided to enforce the rules of play. It is in the provision of machinery and the honest purpose to enforce our conference codes that we have been weak — both at the institutional and at the conference level. It is here that we have our best chance to make progress and to clear up the confusion between collegiate and professional sport. For if we cannot look for decency and honor and sportsmanlike compliance with the rules in a college or a university, established for the training of youth, where in the world shall we expect to find them?

Our troubles in intercollegiate athletics are nothing new. The situation is one that we have all grown up and gone along with unwittingly and without sinister intent. Indeed we have had pride and enjoyment in the growth of a significant American enterprise. Yet the college and university presidents of the country are now on the "hot seat," so to say, for what has happened in intercollegiate sports. Many of us would indeed like to take a hand in the situation; but one should not overestimate the power and influence of college presidents.

As President John A. Hannah of Michigan State once pointed out in a brass-tacks talk about athletics, the college president's tenure in office, like that of the football coach, can be short-lived indeed, and for much the same reasons. Like the football coach, the president is responsible to too many people — mostly people who have only a one-sided and seasonal interest in the university and who, for the most part, actually have no legal responsibility whatsoever for any control of the university.

But they have a lot of public influence. Regents and trustees are sensitive to their attitudes. Only the regular faculty, which carries the long-range burden of educational policy and integrity and whose tenure is superior to passing passions, enjoys the great gift of freedom from fear and foolishness about athletics. Yet the college faculties, too, which have presumably controlled athletics these many years, must share in the blame for the growth of professionalism in college sports; and so must the alumni and the sports fans of the general public, the sports writers who have both lionized and criticized coaches and athletes beyond good sense, the athletic officials and coaches who have compounded their own problems and who have in some cases fouled their own nests.

The current problem in collegiate athletics, as I have said, is not something sudden. Its prewar proportions were plain to see, and they were beginning to be overpowering even then. The NCAA faced up to the problem, frankly and courageously, at its meeting in Los Angeles in December 1939, when the first draft of a new constitution was proposed. The tensions at that meeting were high. Not long before, some of the southern institutions had adopted their conference codes of open and outright athletic subsidies. The Western Conference, on the other hand, had tightened its regulations on recruiting. The University of Chicago had turned from its great athletic tradition to withdraw from intercollegiate football.

By the time the revised constitution was finally adopted, just after Christmas in 1941, the nation was at war. All normal concepts and conditions of competition were soon upset. Many of the smaller schools gave up major sports. Some institutions used Navy enlistees on their teams; others had no such trainees. The trainees, where used, were under government subsidy — and assigned, in many cases, to institutions which they had never previously attended or planned to attend. Eligibility rules were suspended or revised to take account of the abnormal situation. Coaches in uniform found themselves often with the strange assignment of training teams to battle their own former players.

To the extent that all this aided sound military training and helped military recruiting, it was necessary and worthwhile. In other respects it confused the issue of a sounder program of intercollegiate athletics, and retarded reform. The first two football seasons of postwar normalcy — or of peacetime lunacy, whichever you prefer! — brought a nationally advertised "black market" in football players for hire. It was a time of release and reaction from wartime controls in public affairs; of typical postwar disillusionment and cynicism; of coaches and college heads cat-calling like children over the kidnapping of veteran student transfers; of athletic conference cowardice over restoring normal eligibility requirements; of inflation-mad scrambles for stadium seats at any price. Louder than ever — and funnier, too, except for its crazed hysteria — were the shrill yelps for coaching scalps, led by the students themselves at two major institutions, although students generally are saner about athletics than anyone else.

Even more shocking were rumors of players who threatened a "sitdown strike" for a better deal on athletic subsidies, and others

74

who fell prey to the easy-money approaches of unscrupulous gamblers. The week-to-week team ratings, reduced to statistical science, and the regular publication of scoring odds are news interesting enough to the ordinary fan, but surely grist for the mill of the gamblers.

It is perfectly plain to see how the roommate of the football captain or some low-paid rubber in the training room, some privileged fan at football practice or some sports reporter careless of his code, could be prevailed upon to pick up something on the side as a tipster with inside information to be supplied regularly and sometimes quite innocently, not to a known syndicate but to some more respectable alleged expert, found finally to be a "fence." For the more unscrupulous, or sometimes disgruntled, hanger-on, the role of spy has a historic appeal. The college basketball bribery scandals of some years ago should remind us that the possibility of a devastating betting scandal still hovers like a black harpy over the big-time intercollegiate athletic scene.

The mounting plethora of post-season "bowl" games — orange, oil, rose, cotton, cigar, tobacco, raisin, "gator," any and everything but collegiate — is no help in all this. They put new compulsion on the coaches to win at any cost, and they take the game from the campus, where college football belongs. I do not wish to depreciate the desirability of competition between, say, midwestern universities and the splendid universities of the Pacific West and Northwest. We have that now, in the regular season. The airplane has made it possible with no more loss of time than a Minnesota trip to Indiana or Purdue by railroad in earlier days. It is the concession to post-season pressure, colored by off-campus commercialism, that sets us back.

I know it is easier to be sensational than sensible about university athletics. It is also easier to be perfunctory, to assume that "all is well," than to be realistic. But to be hypocritical rather than sincere is the unforgivable offense.

It seems to me sensible to recognize symptoms of a tendency which, unless checked, can grow like a cancer to choke out the clean tissue of intercollegiate sports. It seems to me realistic to understand the danger of just drifting with the tide into depths too great for rescue. To be hypocritical is to lose our own self-respect and surely the respect of all who have the right to look for honor and honesty in the colleges and universities of the country, if anywhere.

No overnight reversal of present trends, contracts, or commitments can be expected, things being as they are. No sudden and sweeping reform could, in fact, be carried through. But we had better begin working our way back to the main road of an intercollegiate athletic program consistent with common sense and with college aims. As on any highway, there are rules of the road which should be respected. Perhaps they should be revised; but surely they should be enforced.

The National Collegiate Athletic Association is presumably a collection of institutions, not just an annual convention or a convenience for conducting championships. Its strength is in the soundness and the sanction of its members. Its historic origin was in the organized collegiate response to a need in an earlier crisis. This association is on record rightly, in its revised constitution, for sanity and soundness, for "satisfactory standards of scholarship, amateur standing and good sportsmanship." It has no powers of compulsion except upon those who acquiesce voluntarily in its aims. As the head of a member institution in this association, I sincerely hope that the NCAA will call upon its constituent members to stand up and be counted on the issue of honest adherence to its constitution. Steps should be taken to separate the sheep from the goats, to corral the men from the mice, to cull the college-minded from those who don't mind having their teams considered as "ball clubs," to use the professional vernacular of the sports writer.

If there be those who prefer the side road, let them stay there. But let the colleges and universities be judged fairly by the standards to which they honestly desire to adhere. Let each member institution face frankly the clearly expressed obligations of the association's constitution, and decide whether it can sincerely comply.

Let those who cannot either accomplish changes in the constitution or decently withdraw, and be barred thereby from participation in the various championship games and meets conducted by the association. Let this association thereafter set up some machinery for the enforcement of its standards, possibly through inspection or accreditation like that required by the best professional associations in the academic world or the regional collegiate and secondary school associations.

Members of the coaches' associations should welcome this advance. Their faculty status today is not sufficiently secure, and their right to full-fledged professorial tenure and acceptance by no means fully won. Every conscientious university president I know would welcome the peace that would come from greater security for the coach as a member of the college staff. Certain coaches, like certain presidents, I suppose, will find themselves sometimes discouraged by a lack of long-range community confidence, and, with a feeling of failure, will resign — but such a circumstance is vastly different from massacre by a mob.

There are those, I know, who think the battle for the amateur ideal has been lost; that the ideal is not practical; that it is silly to shadowbox with reality. You can say that about any ideal — that it has never been fully won, and never can be. There are always good excuses for the fainthearted and the insincere.

A respected former Ivy League university president, weary of evasions and evidently discouraged by some happenings in that conference, once said to me that he feared the fight against subsidies has been in vain. What athletic directors and coaches can't accomplish directly they can connive to get done by individual alumni and other groups, he said. The colleges might make a final compromise, he suggested, on the principle that if an athlete were admitted strictly under regulations controlling all other admissions, and if he then maintained a scholarship record satisfactory for graduation, that would be the most that could be hoped for. In the same conversation he said that two football players denied admission to his institution showed up later as members of a rival Ivy League team. Here again we have the issue of good faith in enforcement—and here again the test is of institutional integrity, not of the written terms of a rule.

The athletic directors, graduate managers, and coaches will be the indispensable front line of any real reform, with the faculties and the presidents in next rank support. Both will be backed up by a very large public and alumni constituency, little heard from generally, but ready to battle, I sincerely believe, for the right things if the issue can be clearly stated and understood.

That issue is the validity of the amateur attitude and commitment. How prophetic was the Carnegie Foundation in its historic and largely unheeded Bulletin No. 23. "The proposal that the amateur convention in college sport be abolished is a counsel of defeat," the foundation declared. "The abolition of the amateur code . . . not only will destroy the best that is now gained from college sport, but would bring with it a new set of evils that would be infinitely worse than any that now obtain." The code has never been really abolished, but it has been sufficiently by-passed to bring many of the evils that were foreseen. It is the lesson of life that evils *can* be overcome — and education shares with religion and morality that obligation.

We have much to build upon. The great majority of the member institutions of the NCAA can be counted upon, I feel sure. As for the University of Minnesota, I want our efforts strongly on the side of needed reform, the conduct of our athletic program consistent with educational policies elsewhere in the university, and open and honest compliance with whatever rules and regulations we adopt and want others to observe. I want men on our athletic and coaching staffs of character as well as competence. I want Minnesota influence and leadership in the Western Conference to support the principles and philosophy of the amateur code, and I want the Western Conference to regain its position of leadership and good example in the American intercollegiate athletic picture. If this means a set of rules which puts us at a disadvantage, competitively, with institutions outside the Big Ten, then let's play round robins inside the Big Ten.

I am convinced that no one institution can go it alone in athletic policy, and that we must have the support of like-minded universities. Constructive consultation among the major athletic conferences can end the unethical athletic scholarship racket and legalize the right kind of recruiting. I am also hopeful that the better universities and conferences will cut loose from the kind of competition exemplified by nineteen "bowl" games — surely the wrong way to start a New Year. These are a far cry from the carefully planned national tournaments and meets conducted by the NCAA immediately following the close of the various sports seasons.

The newspapers, sportswriters, and radio reporters can be counted upon, I firmly believe, to give strong support to a campaign for the best, and no less, in college athletics. Their first assignment is to report the news; and such an effort surely would be news. If the press has been cynical, confused, or careless in the matter of the amateur concept, it has reflected the cynicism and carelessness of the colleges.

Despite occasional academic witch-hunts and ignorance of the importance of academic freedom, the press of this country has respected the dignity and necessary disinterestedness of universities, has given generous aid to their high aims, and has helped immeasurably to underwrite their integrity. The press and radio have built the enormous present public interest in intercollegiate athletics. They can help to salvage its soundness.

But the real work must be done where we live — in our own colleges and universities, large or small. The big crowds are too much blamed for the evil of overemphasis. I have served in a fine small state university, too, in a conference of small schools in most of which the gate receipts were insufficient to carry the full costs of a legitimate intercollegiate and intramural sports and physical education program, and where the regular academic budget had to be drawn upon. The pressure to win at any cost and to cut the corners of the amateur code can be just as insistent there, and just as hard to resist.

The coaches and those immediately responsible for the management of our athletic programs must lead out in the effort for reform. Just as the president of the university looks for improvement and leadership to those professionally qualified and responsible in any area of the academic program — in science or the humanities, for example — so he must do in athletics. But he must encourage and stand by those with the intelligence and courage to lead out. As a major spokesman to the alumni and the public, the president can back up the coaches where they need support the most.

More than this, the president can pull the whole faculty, which has more power and security than any coach or president, into the picture. "Institutional control" should be faculty control. Faculty athletic committees serve sometimes merely as complaisant stooges. Sometimes they are men not really representative of the true strength and character of the American college faculty. Too often they are not really responsible to the faculty as a whole. There is little real public distrust of higher education except in the conduct of athletics, which are too often regarded as something apart from the main purposes of our institutions — "on the wrong side of the tracks." To get them back on the campus is the problem. Given that assignment, made a real partner in that program, the faculty can work wonders.

If correcting some of the evils of overemphasis in intercollegiate athletics means de-emphasis, then that's just what it means. But if it means insistence on the will to win within the rules, not only the rules of the playing field, but the rules which govern before the whistle ever blows; if it means a new recognition of the fine values of athletic representation and competition; if it means restoring ethics and educational significance to the athletic experience of our students — then let's call it "re-emphasis" of some things we have tended to forget.

There should be no need to justify the existence of intercollegiate athletics or to defend their rightful place in our educational pattern. Like most Americans, I am a stanch believer in their value. Yet despite the lesson of wartime selective service rejections, we have yet to develop in this country an adequate appreciation of physical recreation as an antidote to the nervous stresses of modern society and as an instrument for the improvement of public health.

Centuries ago Plato said that "games and physical training are not merely necessary to the health and development of the body, but to balance and correct intellectual pursuits." The mere athlete, he warned, is brutal or Philistine; the mere intellectual, unstable or spiritless; the right education must tune the two strings of both body and mind to a perfect spiritual harmony.

Our intercollegiate contests which are sponsored by educational institutions exemplify this relationship and provide a powerful incentive toward healthful recreation, starting with the student and spreading into our whole society. The greater their public patronage, the more widely learned the lesson will be, provided that the emphasis is honestly educational.

But there is something beyond this that we prize: the shining lesson of sportsmanship; of "friendship through contest" as it is carved high on the stadium tower of my own Alma Mater; of loyalty, shoulder-to-shoulder in the stands and on the team, loyalty to an institution and an ideal bigger and finer than ourselves, to the whole high purpose of your college or university and mine.

We have lived in these last years in a world of broken promises, of treaties betrayed, of dishonor and disappointment, of desperate struggles that know no rules, no mercy, no sportsmanship. How sorely we need a renewal of our faith in human honor.

In just such a time of weary disillusionment, following World War I, the late John Galsworthy, that sensitive British writer and gentleman, said something that summarizes my plea for college athletics. "Sport," he said, "which still keeps the flag of idealism flying, is perhaps the most saving grace in the world today — with its spirit of rules kept and regard for the adversary, whether the fight is going for or against." It is a new summons, not only to the letter but to the *spirit* of sportsmanship that confronts our colleges and universities today.

# CHAPTER VIII

# The University's Public Relations

I HAVE discussed at some length the philosophy and traditions of the state university, its role of service to the state and its people, and some of the special problems it must solve in our democratic society.

There is another special problem for the state university, and that is how to tell, clearly and effectively, to the people of the state the story I have tried to tell in these chapters — the story of the true importance and worth of their university. This is the problem of "public relations," so called, though its seriousness and deeper meaning transcend the rather shallow connotations that have come to be attached to the term.

We are led to ask: What is an adequate public relations program for a state university, and how can it best be carried out? What *are* public relations in the university context, and just what "public" are we talking about? These are difficult questions, to which one might add a still more difficult one: how does a nonpartisan, nonpolitical state university maintain good public and financial relations with a highly partisan and political state legislature? I do not expect to provide answers to all these thorny matters, but we might begin with a brief case history.

The University of Minnesota, one of the largest state universities in America in full-time student enrollment, has been magnificently supported and developed in the more than a century of its existence by the people of a state comprising less than 2 per cent of the total population of the United States. Ours is economically and politically very much an agricultural state. Except for iron ore production, we have relatively little taxable heavy industry. Our university appropriations require nearly one-fourth of the total state general revenue budget. Our total annual university fiscal operations run well beyond $80 million — of which just over 40 per cent comes from state taxes and appropriations of one kind and another.

All this would seem to add up to reasonably good public relations. I wish I could be sure of this, for the demands of the future for public understanding of state university needs will be even greater than those of the past.

We believe on our campus that an intelligently organized public relations program is indispensable to public understanding, and thereby public support, of our purposes and of our vast and diverse program of teaching, research, and public services. We budget more than $90,000 annually, plus many special allotments, for our Department of University Relations. This does not include our Agricultural Information Service, our radio station, and many other activities of direct significance in public communication and relations.

Yet these information programs are only a small part of the total public relations picture in a state university. Public relations must be recognized, first of all, as human relations. They are personal and psychological and behavioral, not an abstract entity — a lesson that some of the social sciences were a bit slow to learn. They are related to many functions of management and policy formation, as well as to the field of communications and information. W. Emerson Reck, vice-president of Wittenberg College, described the public relations of any college as a measure of the prestige of the college, and the sum of all the impressions people have regarding the institution.

But "people" is a pretty big word — and one difference between the present-day public relations expert and the old-time amateur is the capacity of the former to identify the "special publics" with which an institution – business, professional, or educational – must deal.

Sometimes these special publics, or groups in the public constituency, have interests in common to a greater or less degree. Sometimes their interests are in sharp conflict. Sometimes – more often than not, indeed – the average citizen, or the special citizen such as an alumnus, belongs to several recognizable special publics whose interests are inconsistent: the farmer apprehensive of larger taxes who still wants "parity prices" or more specialized agricultural research to solve his particular problems of production; the businessman who acknowledges the indispensability of economic and industrial research but who regards the taxes generally as money down the drain; or the alumnus who demands a winning team while indifferent to the scholarly and scientific pre-eminence of his institution.

To identify these special publics is to compound the problem of public relations, of course. To ignore them is to shoot unaimed arrows into the air to fall to earth we know not where.

The bedrock of institutional public relations, certainly, is what we are and do – and the why and how of doing it. The tradition of universities in our Western world is a tremendous asset at the outset. It carries an almost automatic aura of dignity and respect. But there are dangers in the too-taken-for-granted stereotype. Some ivy on the outside, or even the most modern aluminum fenestration, is no guarantee of the quality of what goes on inside the building. Professors, the best and the most boresome, look alike in the processional cap and gown. A college can be considered better, and better supported, than it really is.

The professional caliber and, almost equally, the institutional loyalty and commitment of its staff are the real starting point of an institution's public relations. Hence, the problem of adequate internal communication comes before effective communication with publics outside the university. Are there adequate techniques and channels of communication and consultation in the complex organization of administration, faculty and staff, and students –

a well-edited "house organ," for example? Are the major institutional policies pretty well understood and acquiesced in, the products of some degree of staff participation? These are fundamental and worrisome questions to which few of us in university administration, I'm afraid, could give unqualified affirmative answers. They carry us immediately into the realm of administration and management as a *sine qua non* of productive public relations.

In business there are many yardsticks used by management for policy determination: those of cost and price, sales and consumer response, measures of the market, the limits and necessities of labor relations, and so forth — all of these involving special publics, too.

But our state university publics, reacting to our institutional policies and management, are more numerous: the special groups of tax-conscious voters; the professions whose practitioners we train; the sometimes fiscally competitive public schools and their constituencies; the groups demanding special research and public services which cost money; the students whose later alumni attitudes are in process of being shaped; the parents; and, always, our own people — the staff, academic and nonacademic — who are the institution in operation and who exemplify to every special public the worth and integrity, or lack of them, of our institution.

The state university's yardsticks, too, are not the same as those of business or other institutions. We are creatures of the legal and political commonwealth, held strictly accountable to policies and regulations designed in a context sometimes constrictive to our peculiar needs and purposes. Some state universities have been granted constitutional autonomy, but this is far from the freedom from governmental interference and control conceded to the British universities, for example.

Our imperative of intellectual independence comes constantly into conflict with the easier policies of convenience and compromise to gain good will. Against the popular resistance to taxes and appropriations, there is the rising floodtide of enrollments and the demands of parents and young people for educational opportunity, with inevitable repercussions on tuition and admissions policies.

President Truman kept a sign on his desk: "The buck stops

here." So does it at the state university president's desk. The "buck" passes upward from within, and downward from the regents and trustees representing whatever public may be specially articulate at the time; but it always stops at the same place.

At staff conferences over which the state university president presides, there are the academic vice-president or provost, the business officer, the physical plant head, the admissions officer, the director of public relations, and others — each with his own problems and philosophy, each adept in the use of the particular yardstick of his specialty. It is in these sessions that recommendations of far-reaching import for public relations are hammered out for presentation to our trustees and our regents. It is the president's final responsibility to understand, to appraise, to use or reject, or to compromise the recommendations of these expert and experienced associates. The yardstick of the public relations director is less exact, in the nature of the case, than those of the others — but his insight and intuitions are invaluable.

In the state university, all of this comes to "the clutch" when biennially (in most states) the decision must be made as to the amount and nature of the university's request for appropriations, along with the most realistic appraisal we can make of the means and prospects of securing this amount. It is then that the university must estimate how much it can hypothecate from the banks of good will among its special publics, drawing upon the deposits built up by institutional integrity and service and by resourcefully nurtured public relations.

I find myself coming back constantly to these "special publics" and the ways to deal with them. People are often irrational about their state university — and not only in athletics. Like the blind man and the elephant in the fable, they discern only its trunk or its tail, and misjudge the whole animal.

Our public relations must be selective, but the selective approach must also convey some contagion of larger understanding, some perception of the fact that the whole is greater than its parts. The ceaseless round on our state university campuses of short courses, conferences for professional groups, alumni reunions, and other outside contacts provides an opportunity to be capitalized in this regard, an opportunity to point out the larger forest of which these or those trees are just a part. There must be speakers at such meetings specially briefed, and literature explicitly prepared, to make the point.

The public relations director cannot do it all. He can discern opportunities, but only presidential encouragement and direction can spread through the countless campus channels the awareness of total institutional integrity as the source of each specialized service and competence.

Its special publics impinge upon the state university in all kinds of ways. Some are close and always counted on. Others seem remote. Some are known to be unfriendly. But there is always the chance for individual "infiltration" and cultivation even among these.

It is a rare individual in Minnesota, for example, who does not at some time or other come into direct contact either with the university or with someone who understands its work and worth: the students and their parents, a member of the American Legion or the Jaycees (two organizations, among others, which are definitely allied in University of Minnesota projects), the farmer reached by the agricultural extension service, the Minnesota-trained doctor or dentist or pharmacist and his clientele, the trade unionist whose needs and interests are being met through special classes in labor education. All this adds up to a great opportunity, if organized and exploited.

All colleges and universities share another potential built-in public relations asset. Our faculties, let me repeat, can be the heart of our long-range public relations program. Good teaching is good university public relations. At the University of Minnesota, over 26,000 young men and women attend daily classes. The impression their teachers leave upon them probably accounts largely for their basic attitude toward the university itself. And certainly the attitudes of students inevitably influence the attitudes of parents, neighbors, friends, and, in time, alumni.

And let me re-emphasize the other primary requirement of any adequate university public relations program — the maintenance of good, sound relationships between administration and staff. Faculty and staff must be kept informed, cognizant of the university's problems, constantly aware of the direction in which the university is moving, made to feel that they are part of the great cooperative ongoing of university life. In a large university, this calls for specialized public relations techniques, for it is rarely possible for the president even to meet all his staff members personally in any given year.

The janitor, the dean, the sheepherder at the experimental farm, the surgeon, the elevator operator, and the scientists have more in common than being on the payroll of a state university. Each is a "somebody" to a lot of people — to a family, to neighbors, to lodge brothers, to relatives. Their impressions of the university are doubly important, for not only does their morale as employees contribute to the university's proper functioning, but they are also potent catalysts in the climate of public opinion — of inestimable value for good or for harm. Staff members too often are the truly forgotten special public of the university.

There is also such a thing as "preventive public relations." The heart of preventive public relations is the formulation of policies designed to minimize friction. No corporation, and no state university, ever went through a year without one difficulty or another. The perennial problem of "town and gown" relationships seem seldom to get quite solved. Or take such a problem as that of "breaking" a big medical news story — making sure that the doctors are satisfied that the facts are right, that all the mass media get a fair shot at the story, that the handling is not sensational. Here, regular, accepted procedures based on a definite policy can pay tremendous dividends in avoiding garbled stories and unfortunate repercussions.

Clear-cut policies covering such disparate topics as outside employment of faculty members, the participation of students in commercial promotions, the releasing of campus photographs, and the sponsoring of university-originating radio and television broadcasts can help to minimize confusion and misunderstanding.

88

Such policies, I believe, if clearly understood by all parties and fairly maintained by the university, are both accepted and appreciated. Part and parcel of the establishment of fair policies is the assignment of specific responsibility, so that everyone knows who is in charge of what. Cutting through red tape and confusion is good public relations. More of this needs to be done at my university and at most others.

In this discussion I have taken a primarily philosophical approach to the question What constitutes an adequate public relations program for a state university? How badly we still need to discover, and develop, a foolproof answer in practice. How urgently we need, likewise, to know what the citizens and taxpayers of our states really want us to do, and, further, what they will support us in doing.

Certain things we do know. We know that more thousands and hundreds of thousands of young people, already born and growing up, are headed toward our state university campuses, expecting without question the same opportunities their parents and older neighbors, their brothers and sisters have enjoyed.

We know that the problems of business and industry, of agriculture, of health and medicine, are never solved in our still enormously expanding social and economic scene — and that universities, "the thinking devices of society" as they have been called, are the main reliance for their solution.

We know that the public economy of our states, the problems of our state treasuries, have come or will soon come almost everywhere to some kind of political impasse. The cash nest-eggs built up by the various states during the war years have almost or completely vanished, even though the tax take of all states in the year ending June 30, 1955, for example, was well above $12 billion, more than double the total in 1946, and a full 40 to 45 per cent above the 1950 state tax receipts.

No challenge of this size, this import, has ever before confronted the state universities in public and political relations. Surely we must summon today our every resource of information and persuasive interpretation, utilize to the full protective and preventive public relations, mobilize our special publics, and exercise wise policy formulation.

Sooner or later, each of our state universities will be called upon, I think, to reassess our assignment, to re-examine and re-evaluate our operations and objectives, to make difficult and discriminative decisions. In Minnesota this crisis has come earlier than in most other states, perhaps — but it will come in some degree in every state later on, I surmise.

And yet, please do not count me quite the doleful Cassandra I may sound. In our democracy people do have a way of working out their problems, once the issue becomes clear. Universities are like protoplasm in their infinite capacity to survive. We remember the depression of the thirties and the institutional vicissitudes of two world wars.

The state university is *sui generis*, an indigenous American invention in the long academic tradition of the centuries. More and more it has become recognized as "the developmental arm of the state." More than any other kind of college or university, it carried the burden of the postwar "veterans' bulge" and more than any other it will be depended upon, and somehow supported, to absorb the enrollment surge of the future.

But not wholly supported, I would predict, in the style to which it is accustomed; and the adjustments ahead offer no prospect of ease to the state university president. To help make clear to our constituencies the large problems requiring civic solution for the ongoing of the state university will be the hardest public relations job that these universities or their presidents have ever tackled. It is a job that will test the competence, not only of the president, but of all concerned in the university enterprise.

# CHAPTER IX

# The Changing Challenge to Alumni

THE alumni of a state university are one of the most important of the "special publics" with which university public relations must deal. They have probably been given more time, attention, and thought than most of the universities' other special publics. Yet after nearly forty years in university work of one kind and another, as a former alumni secretary and now a university administrator, I find myself perplexed and unhappy about our failure to mobilize the full strength of our alumni in support of their colleges and universities in this time of crisis for higher education. At the same time, I am still hopeful — more so, I think, than at any other time in my experience. I am hopeful because the challenge to alumni is a changed and larger one, in a climate of national urgency that we have a chance to capitalize.

The nature of our educational crisis is familiar enough by now — the vast increase in numbers of oncoming students with as yet no comparable increase in funds to provide for them; and the so-called "explosion" of new knowledge and research. It has been documented dramatically for everyone to know — statistically and philosophically — in hundreds of conferences in all the states; in the meetings and speeches of the American Council on Education and our other educational organizations; in the report of the President's Committee on Education beyond the High School; in the

President's messages to Congress on education and in the veritable
flood of bills introduced into the Congress; in the spurious excite-
ment over the Soviet satellites that shows serious signs of boomer-
anging, making a scapegoat of the public schools with the possibility of an upward and adverse spread of criticism of the colleges.

Our job is to respond practically to the crisis, realizing that "our
whole democratic system is built upon the assumption that the
people at large will understand and share the objectives of education," as John Gardner of the Carnegie Corporation has phrased
it. Our job is to discover how, administratively and inspirationally,
we can accomplish the advancement of understanding and support
of higher education, and, especially, how we can enlist our alumni
more effectively in this endeavor.

The question is: What should the college expect from its alumni, and what must it do itself to realize these expectations? Well,
we know what we long *have* expected. It has been "loyalty," to sum
it up in one word; loyalty to the "old school," the Alma Mater, its
purposes and needs. The response has been heartening in many
ways — in performance, if not in percentage. For thousands of
alumni do serve and have served for generations their institutions
with devotion. The American Alumni Council reported that
"alumni support of higher education passed the $100 million mark
. . . in 1956, and is climbing at a spectacular rate." "The twin
goals that the American Alumni Council has set for 1960 — $200
millions in gifts from two million alumni — seem certain to be realized," it predicted.

The council could have claimed vastly more than this, I think,
because in the enormously encouraging and fast-rising tide of business, industrial, and corporate gifts and grants to American colleges and universities, it is alumni who, more than any others, have
been the decision-makers.

More than this, our alumni in the large have justified for all
to see, in their lives and work, the deeper meaning of colleges and
universities. In every community they provide examples of citizenship and civic leadership. Their service to the professions and careers for which they were trained is a proud and valued asset of

our society. Their after-college accomplishments bear witness to the integrity of the institutions from which they have gone forth into the work of the world.

The colleges and universities are the gainers from productive loyalty of alumni to the very purposes of higher education, for "the university and its graduates underwrite each other," as former President Coffman of my own university once wrote. "If either declines in merit or worth to the community, the other declines," he said, but "if either grows stronger and better and serves more nobly, the other improves correspondingly."

Perhaps we need to "think bigger" about alumni loyalty: to expect more than the taken-for-granted loyalty of an earlier day; to explore the expanding potentials of the old-time concept upon which we may have relied too much but which so often has disappointed us.

Have the attitudes of alumni-in-the-large ever been really "researched" with the scientific thoroughness with which our own psychological and sociological laboratories investigate the reactions of white rats, or the buying habits of consumers, or the sex behavior of the human male or female? Do we rely too much on the numerically scarce (thank Heaven!) "perpetual sophomore"? Have we identified the more mature motivations of our alumni to which more ingenious appeals can be made — motivations and loyalties with which the college must compete?

The alumni of American colleges and universities are no select and homogeneous company, as some of the small private colleges used to imagine — and as once, in some long time past, they more nearly were — nor yet are they the "amorphous droves" of the state universities, as Henry Seidel Canby once contemptuously described them.

This is all to the good, in some respects. It is a compliment to their individuality, the development of which is surely a worthy educational aim. Like the professors who trained them, more and more of them are likely to "think otherwise." But it complicates our task, and makes more difficult the job of enlisting their interest, of interpreting effectively our institutions, of conceiving new and larger definitions of "loyalty" to which they can be recruited to respond.

Yet the alumni, despite their individual differences, are still a very special public in the larger cosmos of different publics in our total university constituency; and they deserve to be dealt with as such in our over-all program of public relations. This raises, of course, the issue of how best to go about it, administratively — a question considerably debated. The relatively recent and logical identification of "development" as a third or fourth "estate" in college and university administrative organization has led some institutions to group the functions of fund-raising, public relations, and alumni activity together under a single administrator responsible with line authority to the president.

Whatever the administrative setup, however, alumni work, public relations, and development work are three sides of the same triangle. Recognition of this fact has led to considerable soul-searching among the professional alumni workers to reappraise the tradition and the present-day status of their programs and their special-public alumni constituency.

We must also recognize that alumni workers cherish their tradition; that alumni relations are paradoxically both the oldest and the newest on the educational scene in the tripartite organization of present-day "development" involving alumni work, fund-raising and public relations; and that alumni work is the only one of these functions spontaneously and independently established, and originally self-supported and directed, by an outside special public.

This historical background helps to account for the specialness of the alumni public and its administrative and organizational separability, so to say. It accounts for the really outworn and yet still prized and useful "fiction of independence" among alumni: their function of loyal but critical opposition upon occasion.

The fiction is outworn because in modern alumni work the relationship of the alumni and the institutions is one of indispensable *inter*dependence. The cold fact is that organized alumni activity in this country derives nearly two-thirds of its budgetary

94

support from the colleges and universities. But it is a useful fiction, also, because there is pride in proprietorship in any voluntary endeavor; and because in the case of organized alumni support of legislative appropriations for the publicly supported institutions, for example, an organization independent of university management and direction can be more militant and influential.

This sense of alumni independence cannot be maintained if the alumni program is completely absorbed and made administratively subservient to the institution's public relations or "development" program, many professional alumni workers believe – and their conviction transcends vested interests. It is with peril, they contend, that a college treats its alumni as just another of its publics because they are far more than that – they are members of the family, partners in the collegiate enterprise; as no others, they have shared an experience and an association that gives them a special identity.

But if so, and if the alumni executive is thereby entitled to some semi-independent administrative status, he will have about the hardest job of all in the university development picture. His organizational work and his alumni magazine must support and help to spearhead fund-raising among alumni. The requirements of teamwork, coordination, and integration he must fully meet, whatever his place in the administrative scheme. He must increasingly dissolve the "fiction of independence" by re-directing its energy into the reality of interdependence. Actually, except in the irrationalities of athletics, this is a feasible assignment, I think; and there is a large and rational alumni constituency whose good sense in regard to athletics I doubt we have really tapped.

Ultimately, of course, the determination of institutional policies – shaped helpfully by communication and consultation with many groups and publics, including the alumni – can be made only by those officers and members of the university who have all the facts and attitudes in hand and who must then take the responsibility for these policies, persuading *every* public, if possible, of their soundness and need, and defending them from interference by *any* public.

In this newer context of interdependence, the alumni executive — regardless of what percentage of his program or salary is paid by the alumni or the institution, and no matter where he finds himself in the administrative chart — is confronted with a larger and critically changing challenge. With all the rest of us in higher education, he is in a time of test and trial. So is the whole nation. All of its citizens and taxpayers, its individual donors and corporate contributors, must meet within a few years a cost two or three times its present size for the expansion and maintenance of our higher education enterprise.

The word "enterprise" I like, for that is what it is — with its dictionary overtones of risk requiring boldness, of a productive undertaking and investment. It recalls the history of and the reasons for our American higher educational system, this whole land of ours "aglow with colleges and universities, like a field with campfires of an army on the march," in the imperishable phrase of Harvard's former president, Abbott Lawrence Lowell. It reminds us how much these colleges and universities have already contributed to our national wealth and welfare, and how much the nation needs and requires of them in the world today and in the time to come.

Whom can we expect to rally in the front line for their cause if not their alumni? They are higher education in the flesh — the living exemplars, the interpreters *ipso facto* of all we are and do, whether they realize it or not.

The alumni and those to whom we look for alumni leadership and administration will keep on doing — and doing better — the good things they are doing now. It is a sound and solid job they do, with inventive new approaches to their assignment and a new recognition that the alumni program has taken on international significance with the tremendous postwar activities of colleges and universities in educational exchange and technical assistance.

The professional alumni leaders will work first of all, of course, for the progress of their own institutions. For alumni loyalty, like charity, begins at home. But if it ends there, in this moment of national decision, it will not be sufficient unto the day.

How, then, can we widen the dimensions of alumni loyalty to comprehend the cause of higher education as a whole? How can we remind our various alumni that they *are* a "special public" — not only a University of Minnesota public, for example, but members as well of an educated public with an allegiance thereby transcending single institutional loyalty, and with a new obligation to the larger meaning of scholarship and science, of teaching and research in the scheme of our country and the whole free world?

This "educated," this alumni, public has an influence out of all proportion to its size. In the *Ohio State University Monthly* I read not long ago that more than 9 per cent of the American work force are college graduates, and that double that percentage have had a year or more of college training. In this group surely is the controlling proportion of the nation's leadership and decision-making — decision-making on voluntary corporate support of higher education, decision-making in Congress and the state legislatures, in the myriad grass-roots organizations and associations whose attitudes are the composite of the nation's public opinion.

These are the alumni of our own nurture, the very special public upon whose remembrance and understanding we have best reason to rely. How can we lift their sights to an understanding of and a willingness to meet the critical needs of higher education in the days ahead?

Not by the too common appeal, surely, to ancient athletic antagonisms — nor, more seriously, by any encouragement of the dangerous tendency in some quarters toward divisiveness between publicly and privately supported institutions. For actually our colleges and universities, private and public, have been far more complementary than competitive in their service to the nation over the years, and in these next crucial years, I am convinced, their interests will be indivisible.

We will lift the sights of our alumni by the kind of statewide campaign organized in Ohio a few years ago to dramatize the educational crisis. We will lift their sights by the kind of joint institutional alumni partnership sponsored by the Council for Financial Aid to Education and the National Advertising Council which produced such good results in California and Minnesota and other states.

The alumni can be mobilized, I am confident, if only we can conceive the imaginative summons and projects. Each state has its militia, but in time of war they are all federalized to serve the nation in its crisis. Such a federation of alumni faith and works could mean much in these next years. To mine this new and larger vein, to exploit the thrill of a greater and more generous alumni partnership, to widen the dimensions of college and university development — surely these are the changing challenges to alumni, and to all of us in higher education.

CHAPTER X

# The Responsibility of the State to Its University

THE various responsibilities of the state university in serving the state and its people have been the subject of most of our discussions so far. But there is a reciprocal responsibility of the state to its university. State university presidents think often and anxiously upon this obligation of the state to its university, although they rarely speak in these terms. To do so might be regarded as gratuitous by state legislators, for example. It is not good manners, as a rule, to remind benefactors of their obligations.

The truth is, of course, that the state university president is infinitely more mindful of the university's responsibility to the state than of the reverse. How can the institution over which he has been called to preside discern the long-range needs and lift the aspirations of the people who support it — and then mobilize the means of sound response? How, by example and inspiration, can he enlarge the sense of commitment to the public good which must animate the company of scientists and scholars and public servants who look to him for leadership?

By many means, and by many devoted leaders, these responsibilities have historically been fulfilled in most of our fifty states. In some states — and Minnesota is one — the state university antedated the organization of the state itself. When, six years after the founding of our university, the first state constitutional assembly was convened, the primary responsibility of the institution was restated in terms which well apply to every state university. "It is to encircle about one point," a speaker in that assembly declared, "all the wisdom and all the intelligence that may be within the province of the state to encircle, and to send out and diffuse education through the whole state."

The place of the state university in the whole pattern of American life and in the organization of American higher education has long since been firmly established. I have traced this development in earlier chapters and described the state university's unique position in the history of democratic education. This position is acknowledged and has been generously praised by leaders of the great privately supported institutions which came before, and whose integrity and example sustain and strengthen the state universities of today.

Dr. Charles Seymour, former president of Yale University, emphasized "the magnificent services of the state universities," declaring that "their contributions to the higher learning are of the first order . . . [and] steadily increasing." "This is due in part, perhaps, to the vast budgets of which in recent years they have disposed, but only in part," he said. "They have won their position by reason of their sense of responsibility for the welfare of the community."

"During the next century of academic history," former President Conant of Harvard predicted, "university education in this Republic will be largely in the hands of the tax-supported institutions. As they fare, so fares the cultural and intellectual life of the American people."

Plainly, and first of all, the immediate responsibility of the state to its university is to support it as steadily and as generously as the economic resources of the state, translated into public purpose through taxes, will afford. No state university, I recognize, can enjoy a completely separate estate, escaping the up-and-down cycles of the state economy. But the state university, more than any other agency of public expenditure, does stand in a rather special condition because its funds are in the nature of an investment. The state's return on the training its students receive is the increasing culture and the greater competence of its citizens. Its research provides the continuing promise and fulfillment of greater prosperity and a better life for the people of its own and every state.

Charles W. Eliot of Harvard once observed that it is impossible for any great university to have enough money — and it was insight, not extravagance, that prompted his remark. We college and university presidents know what he meant. There is so much that needs always to be done — things that need to be found out, knowledge needing to be put to use, in the interest of the people themselves.

When a state university presents its budget requests to its state legislature, those requests represent not simply what the university wants, but what with conscience and imaginative foresight it believes it must have if it is to meet the needs of the people of the state. Budget cuts inevitably mean a sacrifice in one or more of the university's functions — a potential failure in one or more of its endeavors to serve usefully the present and the time to come.

Most state university budgets can be broken down into three main divisions: maintenance, buildings, and research and special services. The maintenance appropriation represents the day-to-day operation of the university, the lifeblood of its onward course. It will be spent for supplies, services, equipment, and, mostly and most importantly, for staff salaries. As enrollment of students continues to climb in our state universities, so must the teaching and civil service and administrative staff be enlarged to meet student needs and the expanding opportunities and obligations of research and public service. More staff will be needed, and at higher salaries as the cost of living continues to advance.

Most important of all for the university's service to the state, salary levels must be high enough to attract and retain top-level scholars and teachers. Nationwide competition for able faculty members is keener than ever before, and will grow increasingly so as the student population mushrooms. If funds appropriated are not sufficient to maintain a staff of top-level scholarly and scientific productivity, the value of the university is diminished and the state suffers thereby a permanent loss.

The budget requests for building funds are also determined by the pressure of greater enrollments and new services to the state, not by a wish to build or expand for its own sake. So, too, with the third category of university budget needs — the appropriation for research and public services. Funds so received will pay for the state university's research in agriculture, livestock and crop experimentation, cooperation with state and federal agencies in the prevention and control of animal diseases, the support of agricultural extension work, and hundreds of other services. They will pay for technological and scientific research, both theoretical and practical, that will help to bring new sources of income to the state's economy, and for medical research to benefit not just one state's citizens but all mankind.

The trustees of most state universities believe, as do the regents of the University of Minnesota, that no qualified student who is a resident of the state should be barred from attending the state university. They believe that the state university should be just as large as the services it performs for the people of the state require, and that the people of most states desire the fullest possible educational opportunities for their children, the future citizens of the state. They believe it is an obligation of the state university, and especially of the land-grant institutions, to keep tuition and fees to a minimum compatible with the maintenance of such opportunity, with no expectation that student fees will even begin to cover the costs of instruction or of the maintenance of the institution — as indeed, historically, they never have.

The pressures of citizens and groups upon the state university to undertake new types of training and research and public service far exceed any ambitions of its president and professors, I can testify from hard-driven experience. Yet there is an inevitable logic in these public demands. New needs arise in the changing social and economic scene to which public agencies and institutions rightly must respond. Moreover, no state university can meet its obligations if it takes a limited and self-sufficient view of them. Knowledge transcends state boundaries. Any institution conceived and calculated merely to meet the known needs of its own state at any given moment will be found inadequate and incompetent for even such short-range goals.

The state universities have generally been well supported, and have forged forward. In most of the midwestern states, the public expenditures for education exceed all other types of expenditure. In some states, the tax-supported institutions of higher education require larger appropriations than any other single agency or department maintained from state funds.

But the pressure of educational needs is sure to require even more generous support in the future than has been granted in the past. Within fifteen years there will be nearly 70 per cent more young people of college age in Minnesota, and corresponding or greater increases in other states. In Minnesota state support of the university more than quadrupled, in terms of inflated dollars, during the ten years after World War II — but public expenditures for welfare, health, highways, and other services multiplied far more. I have seen statistics which show that state expenditures for higher education in the United States dropped from 10 per cent of all state expenditures in 1915 to less than 5 per cent in 1955.

Yet surely it is plain that the ability of a state to expand its economy by greater productivity, to enrich human life and experience, to find new uses for raw materials, to create new products and services and markets depends directly upon the improvement of human skills, the discovery and use of new knowledge, and the stimulation of civic and professional competence. These are the very business of the state university. And to all these, no other investment by the state contributes so directly and significantly as its support of its university.

The provision, then, of adequate funds is the state's first, essential responsibility to its university. But money and means alone are not enough. The second and equal responsibility of a state to its university is to give it freedom and a reasonable autonomy, in law and in fact, to do its work. This is an old and periodically troublesome issue in the whole American university world. In this time of great international tension, with the shadow of a sinister and savage menace upon the world and the minds of men, it has become troublesome again.

But as I have said earlier the last citadel of all freedom is intellectual freedom — and freedom is the issue of our time. Universities, through the centuries, have been encouraged by free societies to stand in a special position. Research, and the teaching that flows from it, require not only resourceful investigation and discovery, but also searching criticism of the status quo in every area of human experience. Sometimes this process is painful; in times of crisis, especially so. But it has paid off in the long run. In science and technology this is fully understood, despite difficult economic and industrial dislocations. But the larger lesson seems harder to learn.

State universities, succeeding to and sharing in the great tradition, have felt a special commitment to the principle that "the very life of a political democracy depends upon the ability of such a democracy to correct itself by revising its social and economic institutions," as President Harry Gideonse of Brooklyn College has said. Yet a democracy under attack from external force or subversion is faced with the risk of losing its liberties in their larger defense; and the concept of freedom becomes confused.

In such a crisis, the patriotism of men and institutions can come under challenge without rhyme or reason. Surely, in every state of this nation, the patriotic devotion of the state university to the national defense and the national welfare, in war and in peace, has been proved. Yet in recent years, in some states, university teachers have been singled out as a special class, subject to the suspicion of disloyalty. It is not always well understood among citizens-at-large how delicate and precarious are the conditions under which strong academic morale is maintained. Freedom from excited outside and partisan interference is the first condition. It is a paramount responsibility of the people of the state to safeguard "the free state of their university."

For the function of the university must transcend change and crisis; and there is historical authority for that view. Education, as Dr. M. M. Chambers has written, has come to be considered — both philosophically and in surprising degree at law — as a function of society, coordinate with government itself. This concept illuminates the responsibility of the state to its university. It amplifies and adds to the threefold and historic "separation of powers" — executive, legislative, and judicial — which was the subject of much political and philosophical speculation in seventeenth- and eighteenth-century Europe, was espoused in America by Jefferson and others as the specific preventive of tyranny, and became an outstanding characteristic of American government.

Increasingly, the state university has been *sui generis,* enjoying a separate estate. In those states whose universities have constitutional status — of which Minnesota and Michigan are notable midwestern examples — the courts have increasingly proclaimed the theory of a fourth coordinate major function of the state government, that of higher education.

In Minnesota this was spelled out in our state constitution, making the governance of the university the responsibility not of the elected executive or the state legislature, but of a body of twelve representative private citizens, a board of regents chosen by the legislature.

This matter of university management is closely related to problems of financing, and to policies of expenditure. With the growing cost of higher education and the undoubted still-heavier-to-come burden upon the taxpayers of all the states, the issue of institutional management can become acute. In some states the understandable tendency of state officials and legislatures to seek more direct and restrictive control of the state university is already evident.

In Minnesota, fortunately, this issue was settled more than a quarter of a century ago. In the so-called Chase decision, which protected the independent authority of the regents, the early intention of the founders of the University of Minnesota was reaffirmed by the Minnesota Supreme Court.

"The purpose of the [state] Constitution remains clear," the court's opinion reads. "It was to put the management of the greatest state educational institution beyond the dangers of vacillating policy, ill-informed or careless meddling and partisan ambition that would be possible in the case of management by either Legislature or Executive, chosen at frequent intervals and because of qualities and activities vastly different from those which qualify for the management of an institution of higher education . . . The tendency to sacrifice established principles of constitutional government in order to secure centralized control and high efficiency in administration may easily be carried so far as to endanger the very functions upon which our system of government rests . . . It is in such fashion that the friends of free government may sap its foundations by measures they intend for its benefit."

We should remember, also, the judicial insight of the Supreme Court of North Carolina, in the celebrated case of University vs. Foy, cited by Daniel Webster years later in the more widely known Dartmouth College case. Here, too, the independence and contractual status of the state university were protected from legislative invasion; the obligation of state support of higher education was reaffirmed; and the rights of the people of the state proclaimed "of educating their youth . . . of acquiring knowledge of good morals, which have always been deemed most conducive to the happiness and prosperity of the people," in the language of the court.

At the same time, of course, the state university is always accountable to the people of the state in general, and to the legislature in particular, for the conduct of the institution and the responsible expenditure of public funds. There remains to the legislature also the decision as to what support the university shall receive and, in some states — including Minnesota — the selection of the regents who will determine how this support shall be spent. But the responsibility constitutionally entrusted to the university for its own governance cannot be divided without confusion.

To remember these principles and precedents is to throw light on the purposes of our society, which are broader than their organized expression in governmental devices. They remind us that the state *is* the people and their hopes and expectations, something larger and more vital than its geographical and political entity.

Thus the state's responsibility to its university is sensed to be humane, and is made meaningful.

It is useful, also, to remember that responsibility for education was made local, within the bounds of state accomplishment and community consensus, in our American scheme. It has never become primarily a national responsibility. James Madison's proposal to the Constitutional Convention and the admonitions of George Washington in his first and last messages to the Congress, urging the establishment of a national university, have remained unacted-upon all this time.

Not that the founders or those who have come after them were unmindful of education as the very substance of the American dream and the main necessity of democracy. Their convictions on this subject, so frequently and eloquently uttered, are familiar to us all. But it was to the states that they delegated that great responsibility. The benefactions of the Ordinance of 1787 flowed to the territories that were to become states. The federal aid provided in the Morrill Act of 1862, creating the great nationwide chain of land-grant colleges, was channeled to the states, which were made responsible for its expenditure and use.

But as Professor William Anderson of my own university has pointed out: "The states are not free to ignore or neglect responsibilities left to the states . . . they are duty bound, for example, to provide education for the people to the extent needed and up to the level required by the national interest."

Thus, in the field of higher education, "the state university becomes an instrument of the general purpose," as George Edgar Vincent declared in his inaugural address upon becoming president of the University of Minnesota. "It becomes," he said, "a training place of social servants, a counsellor of the commonwealth, a source of knowledge and idealism."

In actuality, the obligations of the state to its university are revealed as opportunities for its own advance. If it acts wisely, therefore, each state will encourage the resourceful diversity of its university's program and purpose. In the broader discharge of its educational responsibility, it will expect the university to work with the public schools in discovering youth of exceptional talent. It will encourage their advanced education through maintaining tuition costs as low as possible and through the provision of scholarships, where needed, by private gifts and public assistance.

The state will stimulate its university to work, hand in hand, with the private colleges and universities and in cooperation with other agencies, state and federal, to develop a comprehensive and well-articulated system of higher education for all its people. It will recognize the values of difference and diversity among both college aims and college students, while at the same time understanding that the whole can be greater than its parts only in their intelligent and concurrent unity.

The people of the state — and this is at the heart of the matter — will realize and remember that high purposes are exemplified and accomplished by men and women of high character and competency. They will furnish and ensure the selection of university trustees with a strong sense of the greatness of their trust, trustees superior to special interests, persons clearly qualified by public interest and public service. The charge accepted, they will expect trustees to plan largely, to think wisely, to stand firmly as "first citizens," lay interpreters, and defenders of the university's high purposes and function in the larger civic community of the state.

Far beyond anything the nation's founders could foresee, the dimensions of democracy — whose undergirding by education they sought to strengthen — have been widened in this era of world crisis. It is in this context that universities must measure up to their responsibilities — and to that larger challenge, those who sponsor and support them likewise must respond.

There is comfort in the conclusion of such a student of civilizations as Arnold Toynbee that the great forward movements in human societies have been born, always, of crisis, representing fresh and inventive responses to human needs. The responsibility of the people of a state to their university becomes, therefore, as great as their faith in the power of inventive intelligence and informed good will, as compelling as the highest aspirations of the human heart.

108

# CHAPTER XI

# Higher Education and the Federal Government

ALTHOUGH traditionally public education in the United States has been the primary responsibility of state and local governments, it has also, as we have seen, been recognized from the earliest days of the Republic as a national necessity, essential to our survival as a democracy. Higher education in particular, beginning with the passage of the Land-Grant Act, has long had direct support from the federal government.

In recent years, the relationships of higher education with the federal government have become far more extensive than ever before. They constitute a major preoccupation in the American college and university world and enter significantly into university financing and policy. Historically this has been true of the land-grant colleges and universities from their beginnings, but within the past twenty years, federal involvements have spread into the whole academic-administrative realm.

World War II gave overwhelming impetus to this trend. The federal government found the colleges and universities indispensable for training specialized military personnel and for scientific research and development. Since the war, federal interests in higher education have widened and intensified.

Educational benefits for World War II veterans and veterans of the Korean conflict brought federal relationships to almost every campus. The government declared draft deferment of better-than-average students while they pursue college work to be in the national interest. The Reserve Officers' Training Corps — Army, Navy, and Air Force — has been expanded far beyond its earlier principal affiliation with the land-grant colleges, and is now definitely regarded, at long range, as the major source of officers for the active military forces.

Federal support of research, initiated by the Hatch Act many decades ago in agriculture, is now pouring scores of millions into the universities for research and training in medicine and health, in the natural and biological sciences, and for defense purposes — which include not only weapons research but the most basic investigations in scientific fields. The federal government has moved into long-range loans for campus housing, into world-wide support of educational exchange, including the reorganization and rehabilitation of higher education abroad, into the specialized training of civilians and military personnel as well as veterans — all these with highly complex and diversified contract and fiscal relationships.

This changing pattern is significant, indeed. No cliché about "creeping socialism" is a sufficient explanation. The expanding needs of a diverse and specialized social order, which science and broader scholarship have proved uniquely useful in meeting, are a major factor in the situation. The idea that public money should be spent or loaned exclusively through public agencies has been considerably revised, not only in higher education but also in many other types of operation. The privately supported institutions, like private business, have been a party to this revision.

The whole notion, indeed, of organized education — public and private — as a social function has assumed new political overtones. This is understandable in the fears and tensions of this divided world. The spiritual and economic crisis of the Communist challenge, with its educational implications, becomes in practical terms a political crisis. Even in a democracy as contrasted with a totalitarian state — indeed especially in a democracy dependent upon public opinion as the basis of decision — education becomes a force of political consequence. Both the federal government and state governments become concerned with education in new ways and are more and more inclined to take a hand in it.

It should not be assumed that the increasing involvement of the federal government with higher education has taken place in the face of strenuous objections of the institutions, both public and private, directly concerned. Quite the contrary. American colleges and universities of all types have welcomed arrangements to train military personnel, contracts and grants for research, deferment policies on behalf of their students, support of veterans and foreign students, and other federal programs combining tangible benefits with the satisfaction of operating in the national interest. There have been some voices raised in protest, to be sure, but the number of institutions that have declined to participate has been small indeed.

And yet, certain dangers in this situation have become apparent in recent years, and have caused considerable concern. For example, the ROTC, originally a plan by which the Army assisted colleges and universities with their own programs of military training, has now become so integral a part of the officer-procurement plans of all the armed forces that control has, in effect, passed to the Pentagon. The obnoxious "loyalty oath" instituted in 1954 by the Army and the Air Force for freshmen, was one symptom of the change. The Army directive was based on the assumption, stated by the Department of Defense, that these students were in some respect members of the armed forces, even though many of them were enrolled by compulsion under state laws declaring military training to be merely academic instruction.

The Department of Defense also asserted the right, in contracts for correspondence courses offered colleges and universities in 1953, to relieve an employee of the institution from further responsibilities under the contract for "security" reasons without presenting evidence or the opportunity for self-defense. The same right has been asserted by more than one federal agency in connection with research contracts, even when no classified information is involved.

This principle, if applied generally, could carry over into every kind of contractual relationship between the federal government and the colleges and universities — into ROTC instruction, the agricultural extension service, vocational education, even veterans' education, and could consequently affect nearly every faculty member in the United States. Whatever the motive, the procedure was clearly an invasion of the institutional autonomy without which there is no protection against political control.

In another sphere, the financial benefits from some of the federal research programs are now recognized as illusory, especially in universities where concentrations of contracts and grants have stimulated large-scale operations. Since a number of federal agencies pay only part of the cost of the research projects they sponsor, the effect has been, in some instances to impel the college or university to use its own resources in ways that have resulted in unbalanced over-all research programs, diversion of funds from faculty salaries and other essential purposes, and partial neglect of teaching function.

These danger signals, encountered in the recent past, raised and still raise this crucial question: Does this growing nexus of federal relationships mean federal control of our colleges and universities, public or private? It is a difficult question to answer, for the very mention of federal control, like the mention of communism, is a summons to instinct and emotion rather than to reason and intelligence. Our various convictions or prejudices blind us to the facts and impede cool consideration. The issues, pro and con, of government support and government control are not so simple as many suppose. They are empirical, and indigenous to the times and to the nation or state in which they arise.

In one area, the answer to this crucial question seems clear. When colleges and universities cooperate in matters of national defense, Congress and the federal government do control and define the terms and conditions. They tell us what we're going to get — if we want it — and precisely how we are to spend it, in veterans' education, in earmarked project-research, or for some other purpose.

But it does not necessarily follow that *every* federal dollar carries strings of federal control. For proof of this we should remember our land-grant-college experience, dating back to the 1860's — a program of federal aid for teaching, research, and extension, creating a national but not a federalized system of colleges under state supervision and control. This system of federal aid revolutionized higher education in America, extending the range of educational opportunity, making agricultural and industrial training matters of national purpose and concern, stimulating higher education for Negroes in the South, training 50 to 70 per cent of all Army and Air Force officers in World War II, and establishing a pattern for federally aided but locally planned and supplementally supported agricultural research.

The land-grant system, instead of developing dependence on federal support and subservience to federal supervision, has proved over the years a tremendous catalyst of state initiative and investment in educational opportunity and research.

The land-grant colleges and universities have had the longest experience of federal relationships of any college group. Generally speaking, that experience has been a sound and satisfactory one, as I can testify on the basis of administrative responsibility in three land-grant universities. That it has been generally satisfactory is accounted for by two things — the fact that the relationship is a cooperative one between the states and the federal government, with the final decision on the methods and policies of cooperation reserved to the institutions and the state legislatures; and the fact that the land-grant colleges, individually and in concert through their strongly organized and competently staffed association, have steadily and successfully resisted the undoubted, although only occasional, tendency of the federal government to intervene.

Most of the problems that have arisen, for the land-grant colleges, have concerned the federal appropriations and administration of funds for agricultural extension and research, to which the states also contribute millions of dollars in support. Today, for both publicly and privately supported institutions, the horizon of federal relationships has expanded far beyond the land-grant agricultural area. There is, in the long range, the same prospect of a reasonable and satisfactory federal relationship if buttressed by the eternal vigilance of those involved.

There is further evidence of this fact from the later developments concerning several of the danger signals cited earlier. The Department of Defense ultimately withdrew the objectionable loyalty oath and substituted a brief affirmative declaration that satisfies most critics. The objectionable clause in contracts for correspondence courses under the United States Armed Forces Institute was eliminated. At the request of the White House, the National Research Council agreed to study the security problem in government-sponsored research and to make recommendations for elimination of abuses. Congress has likewise interested itself in this. The problem of indirect costs borne by our institutions which undertake federally sponsored research is still to be satisfactorily resolved, but new approaches have been made which offer hope of congressional and governmental agency revision of contract and grant formulas.

These results have come, in large part, from the efforts of higher education itself, working through such agencies as the Association of American Colleges, the Association of Land-Grant Colleges and Universities, the Association of American Universities, the National Catholic Educational Association, the Association for Higher Education of the National Education Association, and the American Council on Education. Higher education need by no means be a helpless pawn in the hands of the government, provided that it is alert and united.

This unity is important for all of higher education, both publicly and privately supported. For the pros and cons of federal support are of increasing concern to the private as well as the public colleges and universities. With higher costs and greater numbers to educate, the larger financial commitments are causing sleepless nights for many private college trustees and administrators.

Traditionally, the independently supported colleges have neither wished nor sought governmental aid. Time and again the fear has been expressed that such aid would mean the domination of programs and purposes through federal control. Many heads of the independently supported colleges have voiced firm objection to the whole principle of federal aid.

Yet it seems to me there are serious breaches in the dike of their position. Housing for veteran students, so desperately required, was provided by the federal government, and federal loans for non-veteran student housing has been granted and accepted. The GI Bill of Rights poured millions into the survival and development of all types of institutions, with notably larger tuition allowances available to veterans in privately supported colleges than in those publicly supported. More millions, by way of grants-in-aid and contracts for research, have flowed impartially to the larger institutions, regardless of public or private identity.

Both public and private colleges have always enjoyed tax exemptions which constitute an important indirect source of public subsidy. Proposals in the Congress to provide federal loans and grants for student and faculty housing, for medical and health education, and for scientific research and student aid in the sciences were vigorously supported by public and private institutions alike. Proposals for federal scholarships and loans to capable and needy students, usable in the institution of their own choice, public or private, have received the support of many private educators.

The sometimes stated distinction between federal aid to the individual student and aid to the institution seems to me somewhat specious. In either case the institution is the ultimate beneficiary. In short, by an indirection becoming increasingly less indirect, there seems to be emerging the tacit even if reluctant acceptance by the privately supported colleges and universities of the principle of governmental aid for all higher education.

If this is true, it would be shortsighted indeed to consider the great issues involved in federal relationships in the small terms of a divisive competition of interest between the publicly supported and the independently supported colleges and universities of the country. It is folly to confuse currently popular propaganda with common sense by attributing to the privately supported institutions primarily the virtues of private enterprise. It is similar folly to attribute to the publicly supported institutions any exclusive concern and responsibility for the public interest. All depend upon each other. Nationally, the distinguishing merit and success of American higher education in the whole Western world stem not nearly so much from its competitive as its complementary character — the balanced diversity of educational institutions differently motivated, controlled, administered, and supported.

Assuming, then, that higher education will continue to be an instrument of national policy, and that the institutions of higher learning and the organizations that speak for them will stand together on critical issues, what can we conclude about the over-all effects of our federal relationships in the past and present, and our prospects and needs for the future?

In preparing any final balance sheet on the federal government's role in higher education, it is clear that we stand in need not only of more information but also of experienced appraisal of these relationships, past, present, and future. Speaking from the operating edge of the buzz saw, however, in an institution that participates in all but two of the fourteen federal government programs which the United States Office of Education reported as providing in 1954–55 a total of $1,074,556,000 — or 28 per cent of all educational income for all institutions of higher education, public and private alike — I see certain facts and conclusions as paramount:

1. There is today no discernible federal policy toward higher education — as contrasted, for example, with the University Grants Committee system of the British government.

2. Federal investment in higher education — the provision of funds for specific purposes useful to the national government, such as research contracts, from which definite returns of value are expected — is not the same thing as federal aid. Instead, federal investment may cost our universities far more in corollary expenses than the grant itself covers. But the concept of federal investment in our colleges and universities is important, notwithstanding.

3. Federal investment, or even federal aid, need not inevitably bring federal control. The axiom of eternal vigilance as the price of freedom has been proved actionable in most programs of institutional experience with the federal government.

4. Private institutions, independently controlled and supported, have long shared in federal programs — with the undoubted prospect of larger participation, but with criteria which must be newly conceived for their federal relationships on the larger scale that seems certain. The NYA, the GI bill, the war-training programs, the large federal grants and contracts for research, for example, have poured millions into the budgets of the private institutions — and in this respect the supposed and sometimes invidiously proclaimed disparateness between public and private higher education disappears.

5. As to state and local support of colleges and universities, a considerably increasing supplement of federal assistance seems indicated if for no other reason than that the federal government has preponderantly pre-empted the sources of taxation and public revenue. The fact is significant that in proportion to all state expenditures, those devoted to higher education have actually declined during recent decades.

6. The indirect effects of federal participation in American higher education have produced in some institutions distortions and disruptions of educational balance and equity which patently require rectification. Federally sponsored scientific and technological research, for example, conducted with insufficient allowance for indirect costs, has sometimes drained general budgetary resources, with an imbalance of emphasis at the expense of the social studies, the humanities, and undergraduate teaching in general.

7. Present federal policies for the stimulation of, and assistance to, research — or federal scholarship proposals which do not aid institutions to meet the cost of these proposals — can be misguiding and abortive as a base for the long-range expanded federal assistance to higher education which seems required.

8. Federal loans and grants for capital facilities, grants for research, special training programs through fellowships and scholar-

ships, and specialized support by now have become commonplace in both public and private institutions. But *general* grants for general operation and maintenance have been made to the public institutions only, and in very limited degree — and, for constitutional and legal reasons including church-state relations, seem presently precluded for the independent colleges and universities.

This catalogue of implications is far from complete — and its ramifying alternatives and explanations far from spelled out, I fully realize. And, too, it requires certain qualifications.

For example, no candid state university president could fail to concede that the instances of invasion of institutional autonomy by state and local legislative bodies have been far more frequent and injurious than those suffered from congressional intent or the arbitrary acts of the federal bureaucracy. The interfering influences of private and corporate donors and of the religious constituencies upon the independent and denominational institutions cannot be similarly comprehended because they are rarely publicized.

And despite the sometimes distortive institutional effects of federal grants (and those from industry and the foundations also, let us remember) for programmatic, highly specialized, or even basic research, the fact remains that the research and graduate training opportunities offered have made possible the recruitment and retention at many universities of highly productive top-level staff and of graduate students who otherwise, in all probability, would never have swelled the sorely needed potential of teachers and researchers which the future so desperately demands.

It is important to keep in mind the fact that federal financial participation in American higher education, while by no means the equivalent of true federal aid, has been of enormous significance when thought of as federal investment in the national defense, in scholarship and science, and in a broadened base of educational opportunity for American youth.

My own belief is that if — in all our diversity and in all the indigenous political and philosophical differences among educators and legislators, government officials and private citizens, and taxpayers — some discernible, sensible, and defensible federal policy is to be achieved, it will require a new appraisal of higher education as an instrument of the national policy.

I think that the growing likelihood of federal aid for the public schools will not solve the problem of the colleges and universities. For one thing, higher education in its outcomes is highly specialized. Its results are immediately useful, calculable, and purchasable — and the American people are a practical people in the expeditures of public funds; they will think of these results in special and practical terms versus the more generalized attitude toward elementary and secondary schooling.

For another thing, we have in this country no controllable "system" of higher education, and we want none. The colleges and universities are different from the elementary and secondary schools in fact and philosophy.

To our everlasting credit, we are unmanageable, retaining the right to accept or reject. We are the ultimate architects of our own destinies because the kind of thing we do, nobody else can do. By the very nature of our job, we cannot be compelled or commanded (and the massive effort of the Soviets in this direction carries the seeds of its own destruction). To the extent that these things are true, they are further complicated by the fact that American higher education, alone in all the world, is a combination of publicly and privately sponsored, controlled, and supported institutions. No single pattern of federal relationships can meet our current needs and historic purposes as it might for the public schools. There is no possibility of an involuntary servitude of support.

But we *can* develop a philosophy and a general policy from which feasible programs can be evolved. Because the outcomes of higher education are, in notable if incomplete respects, practical and purchasable, and because of constitutional and legal restrictions affecting general support of the private institutions, the elements of future policy will largely adhere to the principles of the past. There will be programs to purchase results in the fields of specialized manpower, in research, in broadly construed needs of the national interest, and in defense — programs that individual

119

institutions, and especially the private ones, are at liberty to accept or reject.

I foresee no simple or single solution. But the current cross-purposes and chaotic drift call critically for a new look, for new intelligence and new direction in the coordination of federal relationships in higher education. We need more factual appraisal, illumined by insight and experience, of our future needs and possibilities. It is a new national undertaking that confronts us, in some respects similar to the initial debate and decisions on social security, or the resurvey of industrial and labor relations which resulted in the enactment of the Taft-Hartley Act (regardless of individual opinions upon the merits or demerits of that legislation).

The glory and the comfort are that with such a national debate, and with the attempt to form new federal policy toward the colleges and universities, higher education will come, full-scale and *de novo*, into the national consciousness for what it is, what it means — and what it can become.

# CHAPTER XII

# Investment in the Future

THE issues of an ever-increasing student population and multiplying demands for research and service, of new patterns of federal support and tightened state budgets, and of new debates and dilemmas about our whole American philosophy of higher education — all these comprise the challenge to the state universities in this critical time.

For this is a time of change and of somewhat confused reappraisal of American education from the first grade on up through the graduate schools — and of publicly supported education especially. It is a time that reminds us of Horace Mann's declaration that the cause of public education needs to be re-thought and re-fought in every generation.

At no other time in my own years of university experience has higher education received so much public attention. Some of this has been spurred by the Soviet Sputniks and Luniks, and more especially by the awareness of Russian reliance upon education as a major instrument for the achievement of national and international Communist success.

As long ago as 1956, a congressional report on engineering and scientific manpower warned that "the United States is in desperate danger of falling behind the Soviet world in a critical field of competition — the life and death field of competition in education and training of adequate numbers of scientists, engineers and technicians." Allen W. Dulles, director of the Central Intelligence Agency, summed up the situation with the prediction that the Soviets will have graduated 1,200,000 in the sciences and engineering during the decade 1950 to 1960, whereas the United States will have graduated 900,000. In this context education becomes an instrument of survival for our way of life.

Similar warnings have been issued by President Eisenhower's Committee on Education beyond the High School, appointed to appraise the needs of the nation and recommend ways to meet them. "America would be heedless," that committee declared, "if she closed her eyes to the dramatic strides being taken by the Soviet Union in post-high-school education, and particularly in the development of scientists, engineers and technicians. She would be inexcusably blind if she failed to see that the challenge of the next 20 years will require leaders not only in science and engineering and in business and industry, but in government and politics, in foreign affairs and diplomacy, in education and civic affairs. World peace and the survival of mankind may well depend upon the way in which we educate today the citizens and leaders of tomorrow."

But even without the Russian challenge, the needs of our own expanding population of young people are challenge enough. We must face the fact that within ten years, or thereabouts, the nation's college-age population will be doubled. Not only this, but never before have such a large proportion of our young people wanted — and obtained — opportunity for higher education. Today approximately one out of every three high school graduates goes to college — about one in four of the college-age population. There are over three million young people in college today. By 1970 the number of college-age young people in Minnesota will be 69 per cent more than in 1956, an increase slightly below the national average but posing a problem of serious proportions. We cannot properly educate a 1970 student enrollment with 1960 universities.

For the University of Minnesota, including our campus at Duluth, we estimate that there will be 47,000 students by 1970, compared to our present 26,500 plus. Not only does this reflect the higher birth rate of the late forties and early fifties, but it takes account also of the steadily mounting demand of parents and their children for higher education and the better chance in life that higher education provides. As noted earlier, the percentage of young people in the college-age group actually attending college has gone up one per cent each year on the average for the past twenty years, and this percentage is still rising.

Considering these large numbers in our colleges and universities, it would seem that the doors of opportunity for higher education are wide open. Yet fewer than half of the most capable 25 per cent of all high school graduates now graduate from college. Only six out of ten of the potentially most promising 5 per cent of high school graduates earn college degrees.

One of the main reasons for this loss is that many young people lack the money to attend college, or to stay four years, and there are not nearly enough scholarships available to make up this lack. Despite the smaller percentage of young people attending universities in Great Britain, the fact is that nearly 74 per cent are aided by scholarships, mostly provided by Parliament or local governments. In Canada the figure is 14 per cent. In the United States it is nowhere near even that figure.

One American answer to this problem has been the short-range, partial one of federal educational aid to veterans, and now federal loans for others. A longer range factor has been the productive prosperity of the American economy, enabling far more families than elsewhere in the world to send their children to college. Additionally, most colleges and many private donors provide at least some scholarships and loans. But the most important American answer to the problem of providing educational opportunity has been through generous tax support of the state universities, making possible low tuition and fees.

Even here, however, our record is not as impressive as it might be. In our country a vastly greater total amount is invested in higher education than in any other nation — and yet it is interesting to know that in 1950 the public treasuries of Great Britain and Canada provided larger percentages of the income of universities in those countries than was the case for the 568 leading colleges and universities of the United States. In Great Britain the percentage from governmental grants was 70.6; in Canada, 41.9; in our country, 24.3.

It is significant also to remember that the more than $2 billion required to operate the colleges and universities of the United States in 1950 represented less than one per cent of the gross national product and income of the American economy. We spent far more than this for tobacco and liquor and for recreation — and approximately the same relationship holds true today. Public expenditures of almost every other kind — for defense, for public welfare, for highways — have multiplied during the past three decades far faster than those for higher education.

Implicit in these figures is a new American dilemma, and a new dilemma for nearly every state university. How far can the private colleges expand, or will they desire to expand? To what extent will the state university and the state colleges be expected to absorb the burden of larger numbers? Or shall these larger numbers be absorbed by more junior colleges or other new types of post-high-school institutions? Shall fees continue to be raised? Shall admission standards be tightened, limiting college opportunity to only those who are able to present top-level high school records or pass stricter tests of college ability?

These are important questions. They involve our American aims and values, the kind of body politic we want education to produce. They will test the faith which established the land-grant and state universities, some of them more than a hundred years ago, and which has carried them forward to their present size and strength, their democratic diversity, their demonstrated productivity and acknowledged distinction.

For the support, and control, of education do shape a society, as the Russians are well aware. In America, beyond any other nation, we have believed that education and democracy are indivisible — and we have built our schools and colleges in that belief.

Yet despite our present prosperity, despite the unparalleled American economy and our firm belief in its far greater future expansion, tax burdens, too, are at an all-time high. People, especially legislators, are pausing to reconsider the value of their investment in higher education, and whether to reduce it, maintain it, or increase it.

It is this indecision about the public cost of the proven need and dividends of training and research that presents today's dilemma for our state universities. It is this curious uncertainty of purpose rather than any real inability of our people to pay for our new educational needs that holds us in critical suspense.

Lately we hear more often the statement that too many young people are going to college—although those who say so usually mean the children of someone else, not their own. In Minnesota—and many other states—we hear the complaint that the state university is too big and should expand no further.

The contention is also voiced that we might well turn back to the supposedly more sound and slender curriculum of the New England colleges of the 1880's which the elective system of President Eliot of Harvard and the rise of the land-grant and other state universities long since supplanted and expanded to meet the needs of a changed and expanded society.

It is argued by some that quantity and quality of higher education are incompatible; that the smallness of an institution is the hallmark of quality; that mass education, so called, makes for mediocrity.

It is claimed, too, that since college education can be appraised in terms of money value, in the incomes earned on the average by college graduates, the students and their parents should therefore pay more in tuition and fees—should pay, indeed, the full costs of their teaching.

Let us examine these arguments. They are not new. We have encountered them in the past—and in our discussion, in earlier chapters, of the founding of the land-grant colleges and universities.

We must remember, first of all, that our American society is a *moral* society; that it is premised upon, and keeps on struggling to upgrade, the God-given worth and dignity of every individual.

It is this belief which has aroused, belatedly but inevitably, our national determination to ensure educational opportunity for the Negroes of the South. It is this which prompted the remarkably insightful writers of the Rockefeller Brothers Fund Report on *Education and the Future of America* to describe our society as "the declared enemy of every condition that stunts the intellectual, the moral and spiritual growth of the individual."

The size of the state university is significant not in itself but in terms of the opportunities it can offer and the responsibilities it can fulfill. The University of Minnesota is one of the largest universities in the land, but its ambition is not for greater numbers and ever-increasing appropriations — only for the means to meet the needs of its people. To decrease the size of the University of Minnesota would mean, first and foremost, the limiting of enrollment, excluding young men and women from all over the state. It is the conviction of the regents and the faculty that every qualified Minnesota student should have the educational opportunity which the university offers. It is far less costly to expand existing facilities to meet new demands for technical and professional education than it would be to create new facilities or even to adapt other facilities elsewhere.

University bigness can be thought of in many ways: in terms of the size of a budget, in terms of the number of students and staff, in terms of buildings. But to think of the state university only in this manner is to miss the point, for its bigness in the last analysis must be measured in relation to its productivity. It is in terms of what it produces for the enhancement of the economy and well-being of the state that the university must finally be judged.

Bigness in production is a great national asset, and one in which we Americans take pride. We produce more of the goods of life than any other people on earth, and this is reflected in our unmatched standard of living. Production is essential to our continuing prosperity, and in the total productive process the production of trained minds is paramount. That is the kind of creative production in which the state university is engaged, which it is organized to do, and to which it is dedicated. All the resources involved in teaching, research, and service are marshaled for the one purpose of contributing to the welfare of the state and its citizens. Bigness of the state university is but one reflection of the vitality and the richness of those resources.

Sheer bigness and numbers are no guarantee of quality, to be sure. It is the standards and aspirations of the university, together with the needs of the people whom it serves, that determine the degree of quality and distinction. The standards and the needs are mutually interdependent. Together they become the supporting springboards to greatness. Size, as a measure of public need and demand, is a challenge to greatness and to the support to sustain it.

"Anyone who understands how the modern university works knows that quantity and quality are not contradictory terms," President David Henry of our neighboring University of Illinois said recently. "The institution that is large can also have quality. The institution that is small may not have quality. Quality is a matter of resources and purpose, not of size. It is a matter of standards, not numbers. It derives from people, not statistics."

The notion that the individual and the pursuit of excellence are lost sight of among large numbers is less true in a university than in any place I can think of. For education, by its very nature, is an individual enterprise. No one can get it for you. The American idea has been, as President Eldon Johnson of the University of New Hampshire wrote not long ago, that "every mind is entitled to its own fullest development; and the finest development of someone else's mind (some selected minority or elite) is no adequate substitute." For "the next man cannot be virtuous for us, or see for us, or hear for us; neither can he think for us," he said.

So generous a commitment, so hopeful an educational enterprise as the American state university is costly. This is especially so in states like Minnesota where the resources for research and for the more expensive upper-level advanced and professional training have been provided at the state university alone among all the colleges of the state.

The question arises: What can the state — which means the citizens and taxpayers and parents — afford? In almost every state this is a major problem, and one that promises to grow still more difficult. One seemingly reasonable yet completely specious response to the problem of rising educational costs has been to increase tuition and fees. To legislatures and taxpayers' associations this seems a plausible palliative — and few if any of our state universities have escaped the pressure for higher student tuition.

In 1959 the Minnesota state legislature felt it necessary to require the raising of tuition and fees at the state colleges and the university — for the latter, an increase of $45 for the nine-month academic year, or nearly 22 per cent, the largest single rise in the history of the university. This increase climaxed a trend that during the past ten years had already raised our university tuition for Minnesota residents 77.3 per cent, and 111.3 per cent for nonresidents.

This trend toward tuition increase in many of our states is a repudiation of the whole philosophy of a successful democracy premised upon an educated citizenry. It negates the whole concept of widespread educational opportunity expressed in the Land-Grant Act and made possible by the state university idea. It conceives of college training only as a personal investment for profit instead of as a social investment.

This strange notion — surely strange in the American tradition — that the ability to afford is more important than the ability to learn has gained support in many states. Seemingly it is based upon the spurious premise that education benefits only the individual; that education is a private and purchasable commodity to be bought like washing machines, television sets, or automobiles.

No such thought was in the minds of the founders of the University of Minnesota. Our Minnesota territorial charter establishing the university provided that "as soon as [in the opinion of the Board of Regents] the income of the University Fund shall permit, tuition in all the departments shall be without charge to all students . . . who are residents of the territory."

No system of scholarships or student loans could conceivably provide the range of educational opportunity that the low-cost, publicly supported universities have long made possible. Moreover, any extensive system of federal and state scholarships — which in some measure I believe to be socially sound — will require still greater institutional costs; for in neither the public nor the private colleges and universities can tuition be made to cover all the costs of teaching, research, and required new capital outlay for the oncoming larger numbers.

Surely it is logical to believe that the wealthy will pay in proportion to their greater means the taxes required for all types of public service, including education. But if education is to be regarded not as an investment productive to the welfare of society — if it is to be dispensed simply as a purchasable commodity — then, as a former United States Secretary of Health, Education, and Welfare has said, "all the laws of the market must apply, and we will wind up offering *not* the kind of education we believe to be valid but the kind that will sell!"

Have we forgotten the very reason for the being of the state university? Would we betray the American dream of equal opportunity for all, regardless of ability to pay, to which our state colleges and universities have been so farsightedly committed? With more students ahead for every kind of college, public and private, the proposal to raise state university tuition and fees still further — indeed, to meet full operating costs — would destroy that diversified and indispensable balance between the public and private institutions which has been the genius of American higher education, unlike that of any other nation in its scope and success.

Yet the proposal persists as some kind of panacea, a release from the financial responsibilities of our cherished American tradition. It springs, of course, from the exigencies of distressed state budgets in an inflationary economy and a population upsurge, with the added burden of a total tax structure so pre-emptive federally as to constrain increasingly the ability of the states to meet their own tax needs.

What the people of this country, and of each state, can afford for higher education is not, as I have said, a new question. It was answered boldly and confidently in the birth and rapid growth of the American state universities in the far leaner days of the 1800's.

For "affording" is more often than not a matter of choice — and this is especially so in our country today, with the highest level of prosperity and of gross national productivity in our history and in the history of the whole world.

President Norman MacKenzie of the University of British Columbia put the issue in perspective, it seems to me, when he commented that "when people say they cannot afford more for education, they mean that they value some other things more . . . A particular man may choose a better house; a municipality may choose better roads, street lighting or garbage disposal; a province may choose more hospitals or — ironically — more prisons. But there is always a choice. To say that we cannot afford more for education, in a country with one of the highest standards of living in the world, is just not true."

These fiscal difficulties with which our state legislatures must contend, these differences in the public philosophy about state-supported higher education, are only part of the challenge of the future for the state university. Another need created by the great increase of college youth in the decade ahead is for continued partnership and coordination both between the publicly supported and private institutions of each state and between the central state university and the other public institutions — the state colleges and junior colleges.

It is my conviction that the stake of higher education, public and private, is all one, and that we shall stand or fall together. For this reason I have been greatly concerned with signs, here and there, of a possible divisiveness that could be dangerous. We must disclaim and discredit the myths that are sometimes fostered — that the private institutions are essentially aristocratic, and only the public ones democratic; that the public institutions have any exclusive commitment of service to the public interest that is not shared, in the large, by the private ones; that public institutions represent a socialistic approach to higher education, whereas private colleges and universities are the strongholds of private enterprise.

The public and private colleges and universities have grown

together, two sides of the American coin, with rightful claim to two different resources of major support. The failure of either would change the character of American life, with the loss of something precious, for variety of auspices is in itself a great strength for higher education in a democracy.

In the same way, the state university and the state colleges, junior colleges, and indeed the public schools of a state are inevitably interdependent and their welfare indivisible. Any divisive competitiveness among them can only harm the whole fabric of public education. All are faced with the practical and immediate crisis of providing for many more students at greatly increased costs.

In nearly every state these questions are being asked: Shall existing institutions be indefinitely expanded? What new institutions, if any, are needed — and of what kind, and where? Can there be some coordination in the interest of economy and efficiency — and if so, what kind of coordination? Can it somehow transcend institutional ambitions, local community and political pressures? Can it be voluntary among the public institutions, or must it be enforced, perhaps through some super-board created by the state legislature, concerned almost wholly with finances?

Nationally and in almost every state there have been studies, committees, and commissions to find answers to these questions — some of them governor-appointed, some legislative, some jointly organized by the institutions themselves. Surveys and schemes for expansion are the order of the day. Individual institutions have projected their needs for space, faculties, and facilities, translated into dollars of imposing — and to some, frightening — amounts.

Despite the trend toward increased federal assistance to higher education, new state taxes seem certain in most states, now or later. All the studies point inescapably in that direction; but many of the recommendations, while they concede the necessity of expansion, develop the concept of "decentralization," with renewed emphasis upon "efficiency and economy."

The "decentralization" of higher educational opportunity through the establishment of new institutions — state colleges and junior colleges, especially the latter — is the most talked-of and widely recommended expansionist idea of the moment. It has soundness, I believe, for some states and areas of collegiate barrenness. But almost the first recommendation of the President's Committee on Education beyond the High School was that "new programs must not be provided at the expense of the normal evolution and stepped-up expansion of the educational resources we now have." With this recommendation, both of Minnesota's two most recent study groups agreed.

The menace of decentralization to the state university lies in its appeal to the "logrolling" type of legislator whose home town wants the prestige of a college and the profit from another payroll. Disinterested earlier studies by a commission of both the privately and publicly supported institutions in Minnesota recommended the establishment of six regional or district junior colleges. Today public appeals have been made for four to five times that number, with the argument that they can be organized at far less cost than, and by subtraction from, the planned expansion needs of the University of Minnesota. It has also been publicly proposed that the university become strictly a junior-senior, graduate, and professional school, stripped of its land-grant heritage and its undergirding programs of undergraduate instruction. Sooner or later proposals of this kind will no doubt be voiced in other states as well.

This argument, several times heard during the 1959 Minnesota legislative session and editorially exploited in some local communities — the argument that expansion of higher education could and should be financed at the expense of existing state colleges and the state university — confuses the whole concept of meeting the needs of a doubled college-age population in the next decade. Expansion of these proportions must come by *addition,* not by subtraction or substitution — and there is no escape from this reality short of the denial of deserved educational opportunity.

There will be new institutions in many states to meet the larger enrollment needs, I do not doubt, and a wider geographical dispersal of educational opportunity seems to me sound and sure. But the place and primacy of the major state university must not be sacrificed in the process. The interests of the private institutions, as well, are threatened by the indiscriminate establishment of new institutions.

In any event, the expansion of higher education should occur by quantitative addition, not upon the principle of decentralization by subtraction from the quality resources of the state university. Quality, where it exists, can be too easily and unwittingly watered down by the dispersal of limited resources. Excellence must not be sacrificed to mediocrity. The distinction which it has required decades to attain can all too easily be substantially eroded in a single biennium by failure of support. That is the threatened predicament of many major state universities today. The mere addition of a new institution in some new locality is no slightest guarantee of its academic adequacy or integrity, despite the common community and political illusion to the contrary.

There is another peril of equal imminence and importance about which I am apprehensive. With the rising costs and size of existing public institutions, and the establishment of new ones, there is a mounting trend toward enforced coordination of higher education through the legislative creation of fiscal super-boards, created in the supposed interest of "efficiency and economy," with the single idea of holding down state appropriations.

This development, already adopted in four or five states, I do regard with grave apprehension. Educational needs and policies should be the premises and determinants of fiscal decisions, not the reverse. I would deplore and view with dismay the surrender of decision-making by devoted and experienced lay boards of trustees, willing and able to give time and thought to the ongoing and development of their institutions — the surrender of their sense of trusteeship and responsibility to a group which could not possibly appraise the educational effects of financial considerations alone.

One can foresee in such developments the leveling down of the strong institutions to build up the weaker in response to political pressures. One can foresee the possible invasion of institutional autonomy by governors and budget officers, the downgrading of the primacy of the state university whose pre-eminence has been built and whose productivity has been proven by enlightened and resourceful leadership and the devotion of high-level scholars and scientists over the years.

One possible form of coordination that has been proposed in Minnesota — not by the university administration or its regents, however, either directly or indirectly — is the merger of some or all of the state colleges with the university. This proposal deserves thoughtful consideration, I believe. It should not be approached by wholesale and arbitrary legislative fiat; it is the voluntary approach, the thoughtful meeting of minds, that gives the best promise of avoiding the rocks of institutional and community ambitions and vested interests.

But the state's experience with the University of Minnesota campus at Duluth has been, I believe, a sound and salutary one in all respects — in the pride and support of the Duluth community and the legislature; in the upgrading of academic integrity and of the morale and salaries of the faculty; in a wider range of freedom and autonomy than the earlier teachers college enjoyed. If a similar transfer of the state colleges were to be seriously considered, it should be accomplished with not only legislative but community consensus, and the acquiescence of each college, developed deliberately and consciously, one by one. If so accomplished, the outcome *would* be coordination, and special program emphasis in the different units; statewide planning and control to the end that the needs of the students and the state might best be met; flexibility of student transfers; a better pattern of statewide extension services; and a clearly discerned statewide program responsive and adaptable to state and regional needs.

Meantime, it is reassuring to know that the state legislative interim committee on higher education found "Minnesota . . . peculiarly free from many of the serious conflicts which have been marked in other states — conflict between the public and private colleges, dissension within major institutions, conflict between types of public institutions, and poor relationships with public schools." But in that same connection, the public institutions especially were encouraged and enjoined "to strengthen still more the amount of voluntary coordination in their joint planning to meet the needs of higher education in the years ahead."

The state university will remember this mandate, as it remembers the earlier and still challenging mandate of the Land-Grant Act "to promote the liberal and practical education" of all who care to make the test and trial. There is a parallel commitment engraved on the face of Northrop Memorial Auditorium on the University of Minnesota campus, which I quoted in part earlier: "Founded in the faith that men are ennobled by understanding; dedicated to the advancement of learning and the search for truth; devoted to the instruction of youth and the welfare of the state."

That commitment is to instruct those youth who can, and are determined to, benefit from instruction — not just "certain youth" or "wealthy youth" or even the most brilliant youth alone.

This is the whole meaning of the American state university. It has been a special creation of the American purpose, unique in the centuries-old tradition of higher learning in the Western world. It was a fully intended departure from the Continental concept of training an intellectual elite. It has been the touchstone of opportunity for youth to rise to the limits of their capability, and thereby it has provided the guarantee of a mobile and classless society.

It has bridged the dichotomy of culture versus career. It has buttressed democracy by raising the level of competence and civic capacity among our people. Its research has been an infinite resource for scholarly, scientific, social, and economic advance.

Its low-cost tuition and fees have underwritten what amounts to the most generous scholarship-assistance program of any nation in the world. Any departure from that policy toward the philosophy that education is a "private affair," purchasable like any other commodity by just those who can afford it, would repudiate the whole purpose of a successful democracy premised upon an educated and productive citizenry.

Somehow my faith is firm that the colleges and universities of this country, both those independently supported and those publicly supported, will be sustained to survive the crisis and to meet the challenge that confronts them. Every law and charter of every college and university has declared the nation's need of educated men and women; has declared the intention of their founders, of churches, of private benefactors, and of legislatures speaking on behalf of their peoples to invest in the education of youth as the surest safeguard of enlightened government and a prosperous economy, to encourage learning and the means of education as sinews of our national strength and world leadership.

For democracy, it has been said, "is based upon the conviction that there are extraordinary possibilities in ordinary people" — and the development of these extraordinary possibilities is the very reason and purpose of the state university. To underwrite the ongoing of their state university is the surest investment that the people of any state can make in their own future.

INDEX

# Index